Psalms, Hymns, & Otter Songs

From God's River Otter

JOHN M. REICHERT

Psalms, Hymns, & Otter Songs

Trilogy Christian Publishers
A Wholly Owned Subsidiary of Trinity Broadcasting Network
2442 Michelle Drive, Tustin, CA 92780

Copyright © 2023 by John M. Reichert

Scripture quotations marked KJV are taken from the King James Version of the Bible. Public domain.

Scripture quotations marked NIV are taken from the Holy Bible, New International Version®, NIV®. Copyright © 1973, 1978, 1984, 2011 by Biblica, Inc.™ Used by permission of Zondervan. All rights reserved worldwide. www.zondervan.com. The "NIV" and "New International Version" are trademarks registered in the United States Patent and Trademark Office by Biblica, Inc.™

No part of this book may be reproduced, stored in a retrieval system, or transmitted by any means without written permission from the author. All rights reserved. Printed in the USA.

Rights Department, 2442 Michelle Drive, Tustin, CA 92780.

Trilogy Christian Publishing/TBN and colophon are trademarks of Trinity Broadcasting Network.

For information about special discounts for bulk purchases, please contact Trilogy Christian Publishing.

Trilogy Disclaimer: The views and content expressed in this book are those of the author and may not necessarily reflect the views and doctrine of Trilogy Christian Publishing or the Trinity Broadcasting Network.

Manufactured in the United States of America
10 9 8 7 6 5 4 3 2 1
Library of Congress Cataloging-in-Publication Data is available.

ISBN: 979-8-88738-768-0
E-ISBN: 979-8-88738-769-7

DEDICATION

This book is dedicated to my Lord and Savior Jesus Christ, who, showing me grace and mercy by giving His life on the cross, being buried, and rising on the third day, has washed me white as snow and keeps me in His presence and from eternal suffering in the pits of hell.

I also dedicate this book to my wife, Audrey. She has always supported my crazy interests of canoeing, backpacking, painting, singing and songwriting, and now publishing. She always encourages me to be myself and follow my Lord Jesus. She is unwavering in her love and faith in me and Jesus.

TABLE OF CONTENTS

Dedication 5
Foreword 17
Acknowledgments 19

Otter Songs 21
May '87 24
   "Let the Lord Be the Captain" 25
August '87 27
   "Just One" 27
September '87 30
   "In Bethlehem" 30
October '87 32
   "The Reason That He Died" 32
November '87 34
   "The Triumph" 34
   "The Master Plan" 36
December '87 38
   "The Stable Boy's Christmas Story" 38
January '88 40
   "Many Are Called" 40
   "Arise" 42
   "Clear Like Water" 43
   "I Want to See Jesus Face to Face" 45
February '98 46
   "Celebrate" 46

March '88 48
   "My Lord Is Living Still" 48
April '88 50
   "A Savior Close At Hand" 50
May '88. 52
   "The One Whose Hand Sustains Me" 52
June '88. 54
   "Oh, Tobermory". 54
July '88 55
   "Jesus Is Coming Again" 55
August '88 57
   "I Will Be Like Him" 57
September '88 59
   "The Kingdom Is Coming". 59
   "Children of God". 60
October '88. 62
   "To Move God's Hands". 62
November '88 64
   "A Gift for You" 64
   "I Think Every Day Should Be Just Like Christmas" . . . 65
January '89 67
   "Judas" 67
   "Lead Me, Guide Me" 68
   "The King of Glory" 70
February '89 71
   "Are You Ready?" 71
March '89 73
   "That's How I Know" 73

April '89 75
   "*The Dogwood Song*" 76
   "*Angels of the King*" 77
May '89. 79
   "*Heart and Soul and Might*" 79
June '89. 81
   "*Invisible War*" 81
   "*Children Need Jesus Too*" 83
July '89. 85
   "*He Is the King*". 85
August '89 87
   "*Life Is Like a Snowflake*". 87
September '89 89
   "*Can They See Jesus?*" 89
October '89. 91
   "*Pipe Dream*" 91
November '89 93
December '89. 94
   "*Creator of the Heart*". 94
January '90 96
   "*Carry*" 96
February '90 98
   "*Who Will Be There*". 98
March '90 100
   "*All My Days*" 100
May '90. 102
   "*Morning Star*" 102
May '90. 104
   "*Song of Moses*" 104

June '90 106
   "*That's How Much*" 106
July '90 108
   "*O Galilean*" 108
September '90 110
   "*The Priest Lives On*" 110
   "*Middle of a Miracle*" 112
   "*Mountains of Montana*" 113
   "*My Help*" 115
October '90 117
   "*Just Like Peter*" 117
November '90 119
   "*Old Folks*" 119
December '90 121
   "*I Am the King*" 121
   "*This Is My Son*" 122
   "*He Is the King*" 123
   "*Star of Bethlehem*" 124
   "*Shepherds of Hebron*" 125
   "*Glory to God*" 126
February '91 127
   "*Coming Home*" 127
   "*He Gave His Life For Me*" 129
April '91 130
   "*The Bridge*" 130
   Great Is Thy Faithfulness 132
May '91 134
   "*On and On*" 134
June '91 136
   "*Bound Together*" 136

July '91 138
   "Crown of Crowns" 138
August '91 140
   "Is It Too Late" 140
October '91. 143
   "Sing to the Lord" 143
November '91 145
   "Only When" 145
January '92 147
   "One Desire" 147
February '92 150
   "All In All" 150
March '92 152
   "The Least of These" 152
April '92 154
   "Safe In God's Hands" 154
July '92 156
   "Lighthouse" 156
   "When You See the Scars" 158
August '92 160
   "Gethsemane" 160
September '92 162
   "The Trial" 162
   "Denied" 164
   "Take This Cup" 166
December '92. 168
   "Sending You" 168
   "A Child From Bethlehem" 170

April '93	172
"Next Time"	172
May '93	174
"The Power of God"	174
June '93	176
"Drawn to the Light"	176
July '93	178
"Don't Go In the River"	178
September '93	180
"Lowly Soul"	180
November '93	182
"There Is No Place"	182
"O Great Shepherd"	183
January '94	185
"Ten Lepers"	185
February '94	187
"New Song"	187
April '94	189
"Rejoice"	189
May '94	191
"Walkin'"	191
June '94	193
"Whenever I Think of You"	193
"Wandering Years"	194
"Show Me the Way"	196
July '94	198
"Off to the Mountains"	198
September '94	200
"When I Praise You"	200

November '94 202
   "Peace and Joy" 202
   "Prepare the Way" 203
   "Simeon" 205
January '95 206
   "Carry the Fire" 206
March '95 208
   "Wooden Zoo" 208
   "Hand In Hand" 210
April '95 212
   "When I Am Weak" 212
June '95 214
   "Lift Up Your Voice" 214
July '95 216
   "Love Will See You Through" 216
   "Friends and Lovers" 218
August '95 220
   "Let It Out" 220
September '95 222
   "Alleluia" 222
October '95 223
   "Crooked Nail" 223
December '95 225
   "Paint the Sky" 226
January '96 228
   "Is It Now?" 228
   "Higher Ground" 230
February '96 232
   "Of Songs, Of Souls, Of Hearts" 232

April '96	234
"Nicodemus"	234
"Keep the Faith"	236
June '96	238
"Once Upon a Hill"	238
July '96	240
"Stand Together"	240
August '96	242
"People On the Street"	242
September '96	244
"Let It Shine"	244
October '96	246
"Thunder and Lightning"	246
November '96	248
"The Star"	248
January '97	250
"Walk Across the Desert"	250
March '97	252
"All God's People"	252
"Mary's Song"	254
May '97	255
"Light of Jesus"	255
July '97	257
"Dance"	257
September '97	259
"Look to the Lord"	259
October '97	261
"Give Your Life to Jesus"	261

November '97 263
    "Surrender" 263
    "Shine Like the Sun" 264
    "Everlasting Love" 266
January '98 268
    "How Long" 268
    "Oh, How He Loves Me" 269
February '98 271
    "What Is the Cost?" 271
May '98 274
    "Isn't He Lord?" 274
July '98 276
    "I Will Follow" 276
August '98 278
    "Deep Water" 278
    "In My Heart" 279
March '99 281
    "Answer to Your Song" 281
April '99 283
    "Forever" 283
    "Praise the Name of the Lord" 284
    "Great Is Your Love" 286
July '99 288
    "Redeemed" 288
October '99 290
    "Answer to My Need" 290
    "Every Word, Every Line" 291
November '99 293
    "My Jesus" 293

January '00 295
   "Take My Friend". 296
April '00 298
   "What Was I Thinking" 298
May '00. 300
   "When You Walk With God" 300
July '00 302
   "Lord Change Me" 302
September '00 304
   "Can't Stand the Pain" 304
January '01 306
   "Pray to the Lord". 306
September '01 308
   "Yahweh". 308
December '01. 310
   "Abide In Me, Lord". 310
March '02 312
   "Maybe Today" 312
April '02 315
   "Stand On the Mountain" 315
May '02. 317
   "Nothing but the Blood" 317
October '02. 319
   "My Soul Is Young" 319
March '03 321
   "Who's Gonna Pray for Me Now?". 321
May '03. 323
   "Chasing After the Wind" 323
March '04 325
   "If You Were Me" 325

November '04 326
   "Laughter Came" 326
May '05. 328
   "See Me Through" 328
January '06 330
   "The First" 330
December '08. 332
   "Cut One Out for Me" 332
February '09 334
   "Until the End". 334
August '09 336
   "I Trust You". 336
November '09 338
   "I'm Alive" 338
September '10 340
   "Faithful Friend" 340
October '10. 342
   "Eastern Sky" 342
January '21 344
   "Heal the Land". 344
   "Move the Stone" 346

Afterword 348

FOREWORD

From poetry to hymns and songs, all these arts have left a meaningful and very relevant mark on me and on disciples of Christ, our Lord, all over the world.

Personally, as I read John Reichert's work, which is about his life experiences, it takes me back to a much more wholesome time on planet Earth. I have never traveled the world; I haven't seen a lot of great places. Yet, I can feel John's prayers, in poetry and hymns, which let readers learn from John Reichert's life experiences and realize the power of prayer. These readings reveal John's passion for writing God-praising songs.

As a gifted writer/composer/musician, John Reichert expresses a vivid image through his songs, poems, and music. I am sure it will bless you and bring you into a relationship with God, through the blood of Jesus Christ, and put some extra step in your day and bring you into a closer walk with Jesus Christ. I recommend it highly!

— Pastor Jack Hudgens,
Full Gospel Assembly

John Reichert has provided us with a lot of his perspiration and inspiration here in this manuscript. It is a deeply personal, thoughtful, and meditative set of psalms and hymns, all in a poetic and dynamic flow. There is a depth of truth, worship, and praise, sometimes haunting, sometimes exhilarating.

John takes an honest look at how we can embrace suffering and pain and yet dance with the highest of highs and lowest of lows along life's way. O, the depths of truth and love that flow here for both you and me. It is deeply inspirational and brings you in the moment with the Godhead—Father, Son, and Holy Ghost.

I strongly recommend a prayerful and meditative perusal of this manuscript.

— Stephen J.,
Assistant Pastor
Full Gospel Assembly

ACKNOWLEDGMENTS

First and foremost, I thank my Lord and Savior Jesus Christ. I thank God for choosing me to write down the lyrics to these songs. I am just and earthen vessel in the hands of the great Potter.

I thank my wife and best friend, Audrey. Without her encouragement, I probably would have given up and gone and gotten into some OTTER kind of trouble. She is my bright and shining star. She keeps the compass pointing north. I love you dearly.

Thank you to my sons, Zachary, Luke, Tim, Bill, and Bryan. You are an inspiration in all that you are and all that you do. You remind me that all things are possible through Christ. And to my daughters, Erin and Monica. Two of the most amazing women I know. Wives, mothers, professionals—you do it all, even when you are tired. You inspire me to push on toward the goal.

Thank you to my grandchildren, who remind me that even though life is tough, it is okay to play and have fun!! It's the OTTER way! God bless and protect each of you. Gabriel, Isaac, Matthias, Addie, Nora, William, Bradyn, Hank, and Nellie.

A special thanks to my dear friend Steve Weissert. Friends since high school, fellow trombonists, and lovers of music,

Steve and I have been playing and singing these songs since the beginning, over fifty years together. Music is therapy! Steve, it's time for therapy!

It is said that a song is not complete until it is heard by someone other than the writer. Thank you to my church families that allowed these songs to be played and sung during worship of God on Sunday morning. Timberland Bible Church, The Country Church. Full Gospel Assembly. Thank you for praising and worshiping with me in song.

Thank you to all the folks at TBN/Trilogy for making this all possible. Your tireless efforts in guiding and directing someone who got a D in high school English shows your commitment to serving Jesus!

OTTER SONGS

You've heard of the four animal personality traits[1]: Beaver, Lion, Golden Retriever, and River Otter.

- Beaver: Deliberate, controlled, predictable, analytical, organized, factual, precise, and scheduled, to name a few.
- Lion: Takes charge, determined, assertive, bold, leader, competitive, and self-reliant.
- Golden Retriever: Loyal, non-demanding, avoids conflict, thoughtful, patient, and a good listener.
- Otter: Takes risks, fun-loving, creative, energetic, likes variety, optimistic, and avoids details.

Let's take a family of six children.
Firstborn: usually a Beaver.
Last born: usually a River Otter.
Let's say, fourth born but first girl. The tendency is to be more Beaver-oriented even though they are not the firstborn. They are the firstborn girl.

If there are more than five years between a child and their older sibling, the tendency for the younger child is to be Beaver, even though they are not the firstborn.

---

[1] *Four Animal Personality courtesy of Focus on the Family

Which brings you to me: I am the sixth child of six. I am the last child, giving me River Otter tendencies. My closest sibling, my older sister Mary, is seven years older than me, giving me Beaver tendencies. I am all messed up.

My wife, Audrey, will tell you that I am the most organized (Beaver) River Otter in the world who is competitive (in a Lion sort of way), patient (like a Retriever), and always looking to have fun!!!

I am what God made me! Thank You, Lord!

I was on a backpacking training hike, and God spoke to me and told me to put all the songs He had given me into a book. God said that during the tribulation, someone will find them, read them, and draw closer to Him.

These are the Otter Songs.

Oh, sing unto the Lord a new song; sing unto the Lord all the earth. Sing unto the Lord, bless His name; Show forth His salvation from day to day.

— Psalm 96:1–2 (KJV)

Oh, sing unto the Lord a new song; for He hath done marvelous things; his right hand, and His holy arm, have gotten Him the victory. The Lord hath made known His salvation; His righteousness hath he openly shown in the sight of nations. He hath remembered His mercy and His truth toward the house of Israel; all the ends of the earth have seen the salvation of our

God. Make a joyful noise unto the Lord, all the earth; make a loud noise, and rejoice, and sing praise. Sing unto the Lord with the harp, with the harp, and the voice of a psalm. With trumpets and sound of cornet make a joyful noise before the Lord, the King. Let the sea roar, and the fullness thereof; the world, and they that dwell therein. Let the floods clap their hands; let the hills be joyful together before the Lord; for He cometh to judge the earth; with righteousness shall He judge the world, and the peoples with equity.

— Psalm 98:1–9 (KJV)

MAY '87

Captain: *noun. One who commands, leads, or guides others, especially the officer in command of a ship, aircraft, or spacecraft.*

— American Heritage Dictionary

In May of 1987, while on a 1200-mile solo canoe trip around the state of Indiana, I had a long talk with my God. I was thirty-three years old. Two friends of mine, one thirty-two and one thirty-four, recently and suddenly passed away, leaving me feeling that if I too was to pass, what significance had my life been? What would my children remember me for? Leading to the next question: How could I serve my God with meaning? A lot of times, it would be easier if God would just tell me what to do; I'd gladly do it. I'm of German/Welsh descent, and that means pretty stubborn. My wife would say A LOT STUBBORN. God probably does just tell me what to do, but I'm usually not listening. Then, wham, that 2x4 upside of the head; are you listening now?

I didn't really have many skills. I had been a pharmacist for nine years and felt like I was serving God in this capacity just fine. I liked to canoe and had been backpacking since 1977. But what if I died suddenly? The only other skill I had was music, which had always been with me since singing "Jesus Loves

Me" at church when I was three years old. It was more like a hobby. I'm not professionally trained in music, although I have taught myself to play a little guitar, bass, and piano. Enough that I can entertain myself. So, I talked with God for days, as this canoe trip took twenty-seven days to complete, and the conclusion of the conversation was I would write down one song a month for His praise and glory if God would give them to me. It was a promise I meant to keep!

Somewhere on the southern half of the Wabash River, the first song came to me. May 1987 song… "Let the Lord Be the Captain."

"Let the Lord Be the Captain"

Let the Lord be the Captain of your boat,
Let the Lord be the Captain of your boat,
His course is straight and true, harbors safe for me and you,
Let the Lord be the Captain of your boat.

Let the Lord be the Shepherd of your flock,
Let the Lord be the Shepherd of your flock,
He will slay the lion and bear; He'll protect you everywhere,
Let the Lord be the Shepherd of your flock.

> *When you're out on the ocean and you're feeling tossed about,*
> *When the sky is dark and stormy, and the way is filled with doubt,*
> *I've a friend who can guide you; His name can clear a cloudy day.*
> *Jesus, sweet Jesus, the one and only way.*

Let the Lord be the Captain of your life,
Let the Lord be the Captain of your life,
Your needs He will provide if on His word you will rely,
Let the Lord be the Captain of your life.

> *When you're out on the ocean and you're feeling tossed about,*
> *When the sky is dark and stormy, and the way is filled with doubt,*
> *I've a friend who can guide you; His name can clear a cloudy day.*
> *Jesus, sweet Jesus, the one and only way.*

Let the Lord be the Captain of your life,
Let the Lord be the Captain of your life,
He died to set men free, gave His life for you and me;
Let the Lord be the Captain of your life.

AUGUST '87

I successfully completed the solo canoe trip and raised a little money for the American Heart Association in the process. In May, God gave me no songs. June and July came and went with no songs. What had happened to the promise I had made to God? Was it like all the New Year's resolutions that we so often make and never keep? I wanted this to be different; I really wanted this to honor God.

Then in August of 1987, God gave me song number 2: "Just One."

"Just One"

Just one, Holy heavenly Father.
Just one, Son sent from above.
Just one, world of worthless sinners.
Just one gift, the gift of love.
Just one, promise set in heaven.
Just one, rainbow up above.
Just one, Lamb upon the altar.
Just one gift, the gift of love.

Do you believe God would have sent His Son to die on Calvary's tree
If the world had just one sinner, a wretched soul like me?
Would the angels cry Hosanna if He brought just one soul home?

Would He have thought it just a bother and left just one alone?

Just one Land, His chosen people,
Just one man to lead them free,
Just one boy who slew the giant,
Just one King, from Him would be His seed,
Just one Mother Virgin Mary,
Just one night, as cold as it could be,
Just one star by which to follow,
Just one gift, the Christ child, it was He.

Do you believe God would have sent His Son to die on Calvary
If the world had just one sinner, a wretched soul like me?
Would the angels cry Hosanna if He brought just one soul home?
Would He have thought it just a bother and left just one alone?

Just one disciple to deny Him,
Just one who believed upon the cross,
Just one disciple who would doubt Him,
Because of doubt, how many souls are lost?

Do you believe God would have sent His Son to die on Calvary's
*   tree*
If the world had just one sinner, a wretched soul like me?
Would the angels cry Hosanna if He brought just one soul home?
Would He have thought it just a bother and left just one alone?

And I thank the Lord in heaven that He doesn't work that way,
A single child means just as much as a multitude by the bay,
And His love is meant for everyone; His power will set them free,
His saving grace is all-encompassing, meant for millions and just
*   for me.*

*So, I know God would have sent His Son to die on Calvary
If the world had just one sinner, a wretched soul like me,
And the angels would cry Hosanna as He brought just one soul home
To spend eternity with Jesus, just one Shepherd, just one foal.*

SEPTEMBER '87

Christmas time is one of my favorite times of the year, not because of the presents, although I like them as much as the next person, but because of all the focus on Jesus. In college, the guys I hung out with would sit around and take old traditional Christmas carols and re-write the lyrics…none of which can be repeated here. God forgave me for that! I always wanted to write a Christmas song, and God gave me this song in September 1987: "In Bethlehem."

"In Bethlehem"

The night was cold; there was frost in the air,
Then a bright star appeared to guide them.
A shepherd boy alone with his sheep,
Awoke from his sleep the angels near him.

Go to Bethlehem, the Messiah to greet,
Go to Bethlehem, to the end of the street,
Wrapped in swaddling clothes, in a manger, He waits,
Go to Bethlehem and sing Him His praise,
Allelu, Alleluia Amen. Alleluia, Allelu Amen.

Far away near the Orient Sea,
There were wise men three, watching stars.
As foretold by the prophets of old,
They brought incense and gold from afar.

To Bethlehem, the Messiah to greet,
To Bethlehem, to the end of the street,
Wrapped in swaddling clothes, in a manger, He waits,
Go to Bethlehem and sing Him His praise,
Allelu, Alleluia Amen. Alleluia, Allelu Amen.

Today's the day that the Savior is born,
To a world full of scorn, He came to save.
So, gather 'round and place knee on the ground,
Raise your voices in sound and praise His name.

In Bethlehem, the Messiah we greet,
In Bethlehem, at the end of the street,
Wrapped in swaddling clothes, in a manger, He waits,
In Bethlehem, we sing Him His praise,
Allelu, Alleluia Amen. Alleluia, Allelu Amen.

John M. Reichert

OCTOBER '87

I was reading a book by Shad O'Shea titled *Just for the Record*, a comprehensive book about the multi-billion-dollar music business, and it was telling me that a good song either embarrasses a person or makes a person cry. I wrote "The Reason That He Died" in October 1987. When I sang this song for my mom, she sat there and cried. It must be a good song, according to Shad! I thank God that He chose me to write down this song. October 1987 song…

"The Reason That He Died"

Praise His name, holy name, shout Hosanna from on high.
King of Kings, Lord of Lords, I'm the reason that He died.
He came to earth so long ago to relay the Father's plan,
But He was mocked and spit upon, like some ordinary man.

> *Had I been there, I would have slain the Roman guards*
> *To free the King who came to save.*
> *Yet He would prefer to them should come no harm,*
> *For loving was His way.*

What was the charge? What law was broke to treat the King of
  Jews this way?
Nailed and hanged on a wooden cross in the middle of the day,

"Not My will, but Thine be done," He was heard to speak.
"It is finished," then the sky grew dark, and the earth began to quake.

> He could have called upon a mighty heavenly host
> To lift Him up from the cross.
> He chose to wear a crown of thorns for everyone
> And Himself pay all the cost.

He bore the sins of all mankind, of all ages, of all times,
And even though I was not present there, I'm the reason that He died.
My sins nailed His hands; they nailed His feet; they thrust the sword into His side.
Even though I was not present there, I'm the reason that He died.

> And I will sing it from the highest mountaintop,
> The ocean deep, the valley wide.
> I will tell the world about His wondrous Love
> And the reason that He died,
> I will tell the world about His wondrous Love
> And the reason that He died.

John M. Reichert

NOVEMBER '87

John 12:12–54 speaks about Jesus' triumphant entry into Jerusalem. Even the disciples believed Jesus had come to overthrow the Roman government and set up His eternal kingdom here on earth. This caused Jesus to sorrow inside His heart for Israel because they really had not accepted Him as the Messiah. In November 1987, God gave me "The Triumph." I don't know why God gave me so many Easter songs going into the Christmas season.

"The Triumph"

He is coming... I can see Him... Jesus of Nazareth... Lord of Lords... King of Kings.

Go ye now into Bethany and bring me the tied-up colt,
Bring it for your master's ride, cover it with your cloaks
That I may ride to Jerusalem, King over all the Kings,
Go ye now into Bethany, do ye all these things.

See now how they honor Him, Hosanna come to save,
Laying down before Him, palm branches in His way,
Entering Jerusalem for the Passover Feast,
Entering, Triumphantly, let His praises ring.

> *Lord of Lords... He is Wonderful.*
> *King of Kings... He is Glorious.*

> *Lord of Lords… He is Marvelous.*
> *King of Kings… In the Highest.*

On the tenth of Nisan, a sacrifice is chosen.
Young and blameless, it must be, chosen from the foal.
Jesus is the sacrifice to save the world from sin,
And even as they honored Him, He sorrowed deep within.

> *And He cried for Israel, but they did not know why*
> *For this same Jesus was on His way to die,*
> *And the same ones who exulted Him would soon turn their eyes*
> *From this same Jesus and cry, crucify.*

So, He was the sacrifice and died upon the tree
That we might live forever, He died for you and me.
Death—it could not conquer Him—He rose on the third day;
The tomb had lost its power over Him, risen from the grave

Keep your eyes turned skyward, for the hour has not yet come
When He'll return in glory and gather everyone,
And every knee before Him will bow eternally
When He comes victorious, reigning triumphantly as…

> *Lord of Lords… He is Wonderful.*
> *King of Kings… He is Glorious.*
> *Lord of Lords… He is Marvelous.*
> *King of Kings… In the Highest.*

John M. Reichert

November 1987 was the first month that God gave me multiple songs to scribe. Again, I was hoping for a Christmas song but out came "The Master Plan." This was the favorite song of my friend, who played in our Christian band Crooked Nail. But he used to say, "I like them all." November 1987 song… "The Master Plan."

"The Master Plan"

You've heard the one about the man who built his house upon the sand,
And when the waters rose, it washed away.
Have you heard about the wise man too? He was not a joke or fool.
He built his house upon the Master Plan.

> *And when the rains came down*
> *and the floods rose high,*
> *What a firm foundation he had!*
> *Jesus kept him high and dry.*

If you're setting out to build your life in a world that's full of toil and strife,
It's essential that you make a solid start.
A blueprint's where you should begin; it will show you all the outs and ins,
And Jesus is the greatest plan by far.

> *He is the Master Plan,*
> *drawn by the Holy Father's hand.*
> *He'll light your life with hope everlasting—*
> *Jesus is the Master Plan.*

If you feel confused and lost,
Just remember it was paid for at the cross.

So don't be like the worldly man and build your life on earthly sands,
For someday, it will all be battered down.
Build your life on Jesus Christ, the one who came and paid the price,
And set your life upon the higher ground.

He is the Master Plan, drawn by the Holy Father's hand,
And when He comes again to reign,
Upon the Rock, your House will stand,
For Jesus is the Master Plan.

John M. Reichert

DECEMBER '87

My second Christmas song, and this one in December!! December 1987. There are many stories in the Bible about the birth of Christ. In this song, there was a stable boy present at the birth. He is now grown, and his son is asking him to re-tell the story of what he had seen on that blessed night. December 1987 song… "The Stable Boy's Christmas Story."

"The Stable Boy's Christmas Story"

Tell me, Father, that story you know, how a woman and a man came out of the cold,
How they could find no room at the inn, it was the time of tax in Bethlehem.
Tell me, Father, that story of old, about the day the Christ child was born,
Tell me how you saw it—a poor stable boy, on that blessed morn.

> *Tell me, Father, how the shepherds came and bowed before the Savior's bed,*
> *Tell me how the star moved from the east and shone brightly overhead.*

Tell me again how the rich men came, bringing gifts they carried so far,
Tell me again how the angels proclaimed, "Son of God," "Bright Morning Star."

> *Tell me, Father, how they named Him Jesus like the prophets said that they would,*
> *Tell me how the animals bowed to the ground like they knew that they should.*

Tell me why the King wanted Him dead, afraid of losing his crown,
Tell me how the shepherds covered their heads and fell face to the ground.
Tell me how the angels sang with one voice, "Peace on earth, good-will to men,
Go ye now and worship the King, you will find Him in Bethlehem."

> *Tell me, Father, how the shepherds came and bowed before the Savior's bed,*
> *Tell me how the star moved from the east and shone brightly overhead,*
> *For today in the city of David is born a Savior, which is Christ the Lord,*
> *Proclaim Him as King, let the anthems ring, for Jesus Christ the Lord.*

Tell me again that Christmas story of old.

John M. Reichert

JANUARY '88

January 1988 surprised me with four songs in one month. That seems like a lot to me, but I read somewhere that Dolly Parton, who has written over 5,000 songs, wrote ninety-nine in one day!

January 1988 started with "Many Are Called," then came "Arise," followed by "Clear Like Water," and ended with "I Want to See Jesus, Face to Face."

"Many Are Called"

The feast is being readied; the prince is to be wed,
The fatlings have been slaughtered, the guest list shall be read.
So many have been bidden to share the wedding feast,
From the rich man to the poor man, from the most unto the least.

> *For many are called, but few are chosen*
> *To be the ones who will live forever more.*
> *Many are called, but few are chosen*
> *To be the ones who will live with Jesus forever more, forever more.*

The King has sent His servants to gather those who'd come,
So many had excuses, they could not find a-one.
One's family had the fever; they could not be left alone.
Another one was busy tending all the land he owned.

The King could not contain His wrath; His anger kindled hot,
He destroyed all who disobeyed, casting fate with the wife of Lot.
With the bidden found unworthy, the servants tried again,
Asking all upon the highway that many should come in,

> *For many are called, but few are chosen*
> *To be the ones who will live forever more.*
> *Many are called, but few are chosen*
> *To be the ones who will live with Jesus forever more, forever more.*

> *But it's not enough to just show up in answer to His call,*
> *If your robe is not the wedding robe, you'll be ushered from the hall.*
> *For such is the kingdom of heaven, when the Prince of Peace shall wed,*
> *Will your name be on the guest list when the Book of Life is read?*

The feast is being readied, the Prince is to be wed,
The fatlings have been slaughtered, the guest list shall be read.
So many have been bidden to share the wedding feast,
From the rich man to the poor man, from the most unto the least.

> *For many are called, but few are chosen*
> *To be the ones who will live forever more.*
> *Many are called, but few are chosen*
> *To be the ones who will live with Jesus forever more, forever more.*

John M. Reichert

Then another Easter song: "Arise." My friend Steve, who plays bass, said we were playing this song at a church, and all of a sudden, the Holy Spirit touched him on the inside, and he almost started shouting out loud during the song! I told Steve he should have—don't hold the Spirit back!!!

"Arise"

God rolled the stone away; He opened up the grave,
He fulfilled the Holy Scripture with one word that He did say.
Arise, seed of Abraham, come forth from death's dark hold,
Arise ye lamb of God and ascend unto thy throne.

> *Arise, Messiah, Son of God,*
> *Arise, Emmanuel, the same,*
> *Arise, Arise, all ye Israel,*
> *And praise His name.*

God gave the greatest gift of love. He sent His Son
To die a cursed death that the church might live as one.
And all who will believe in Him shall never pass away,
And those asleep in death will awake one glorious day.

> *Arise, Messiah, Son of God,*
> *Arise, Emmanuel, the same,*
> *Arise, Arise all ye Israel,*
> *And praise His name.*

> *Too long we've waited shackled by sin*
> *To open up our heart's door and ask Jesus to come in.*
> *He'll loose the chains that bind us, for Jesus is the key,*
> *And you shall know the Truth, and the Truth shall set you free.*

God rolled the stone away; He opened up the grave,
Now we can live forever, since that blessed day.
Arise, seed of Abraham, resurrection to proclaim,
Arise, all ye Israel, and praise His holy name.

> *Arise, Messiah, Son of God,*
> *Arise, Emmanuel, the same,*
> *Arise, arise all ye Israel,*
> *And praise His holy name.*

My good friend Steve Weissert (same Steve as above) plays the upright bass, as well as the electric bass. Steve loves a good bluegrass-style song, and he loves "Clear Like Water."

"Clear Like Water"

Clear like water, from red like crimson, that's what His blood has done for me,
He made me clear like water, from red like crimson, His blood has washed my spirit clean.
Oh, what a day, what a wonderful day when He set my soul to sing!
He made me clear like water, from red like crimson, His blood has washed my spirit clean

Green are the pastures where He shall feed us when we reach the promised land,
Joy and singing shall be there to greet us when we walk with the Savior hand in hand.

Oh, what a day, what a wonderful day when we cross old Jordan's flow!
Green are the pastures where He shall lead us when we reach the other shore.

> Peace like a river is flowing abundantly
> For all who wish to partake.
> Narrow and straight is the path we must follow
> To reach the kingdom's gate.

Gold and silver are the streets of the city, where we will walk with the King,
A choir of saints shall praise His name with glory when everyone shall sing,
Oh, what a day, what a wonderful day when we sing Hosanna evermore!
Gold and silver are the streets of the city, where we will walk forever more.

Clear like water from red like crimson, that's what His blood has done for me,
He made me clear like water from red like crimson; His blood has washed my spirit clean,
His blood has washed my spirit clean; Christ's blood has washed my spirit clean.

The final song for January 1988, which I had the privilege to sing at a wake, is "I Want to See Jesus Face to Face." God has allowed me to backpack in many of our national parks. There is a campsite in Glacier National Park, Montana, called Fifty

Mountain. When at this site, if you turn 360 degrees, you can count fifty mountain peaks. I stood there in *awe* of my God.

"I Want to See Jesus Face to Face"

When I look into the night sky and behold God's awesome works,
I'm reminded of the beauty of my Lord.
I've seen it in the forest beside a babbling brook,
Yet there's something that my eyes desire much more.

> *I want to see Jesus face to face. I want to gaze into His tender eyes.*
> *I want to touch the brow where the Roman guards*
> *Forced the thorns into their place;*
> *I want to see Jesus face to face.*

I've seen God's handiwork from Fifty Mountain high
In the ocean, as it strains against the shore.
His beauty's in the elderly and in the baby's cry;
Still, there's one thing that my eyes desire much more.

> *I want to see Jesus face to face. I want to gaze into His tender eyes.*
> *I want to touch the brow where the Roman guards*
> *Forced the thorns into their place;*
> *I want to see Jesus face to face.*

And I know I'll spend eternity walking by my Savior's side,
Yet there is something in the feeling that I'll never realize:
Until I see Jesus face to face. Until I can gaze into His tender eyes,
Until I can touch the brow where the Roman guards
Forced the thorns into their place;
Until I see Jesus face to face. I want to see Jesus face to face.

John M. Reichert

FEBRUARY '98

Came down with Mono!!! Doc says somebody who was contagious probably coughed, and I walked through the droplets and breathed them in!! It is a real butt kicker. Spent most of my time in bed resting. I did manage to scribe this song for God while sick.

> *This is the day which the Lord hath made; we will rejoice and be glad in it.*
>
> — Psalm 118:24, KJV

> *Let the heavens rejoice, and let the earth be glad; let the sea roar, and the fulness thereof. Let the field be joyful, and all that is therein: then shall all the trees of the wood rejoice.*
>
> — Psalm 96:11–12, KJV

"Celebrate"

Celebrate, Celebrate,
Celebrate, Celebrate the Day.
Celebrate, Celebrate,
Celebrate, Celebrate the Day.

Today is the day the Lord has made; let us rejoice and in it be glad.
Let the sea roar and the heavens awake; let the earth be glad.

Celebrate, Celebrate,
Celebrate, Celebrate the Day.
Celebrate, Celebrate,
Celebrate, Celebrate the Day.

The glory of the Lord shall endure forever, the Lord shall rejoice in His way,
Then shall all the trees rejoice in the forest, in Thy name they shall rejoice all-day.

Celebrate, Celebrate,
Celebrate, Celebrate the Day.
Celebrate, Celebrate,
Celebrate, Celebrate the Day.

Even if it's raining or the snow is falling down,
No need to be grumbling, no need to wear a frown.
Every little raindrop is a tiny seed that grows a mighty ocean, that grows a mighty tree—
Celebrate, Celebrate, Celebrate, Celebrate the Day.

John M. Reichert

MARCH '88

Not very much happening. I was looking through what happened in March of 1988, and Reba McEntire and Randy Travis won awards in country music. Mike Tyson defended his boxing title. NASA launched another satellite into space, and President Ronald Reagan had his veto of a civil rights bill overturned by Congress. Through it all, Jesus is still on the throne. God gave me March 1988 song… "My Lord Is Living Still."

"My Lord Is Living Still"

I knew a man named Jesus; while He taught here on earth,
He was such a simple man, growing up from birth.
He had so much to offer, He had so much that He could give,
But His Father God in Heaven gave Him the choice to die or live.

> *He had to die, the choice was His,*
> *He chose to die that we might live.*
> *He always forsook Himself, He did His Father's will,*
> *And, in my heart, I know—my Lord is living still.*

He taught us so many lessons, He taught us how we should love,
He talked about a coming kingdom when He'd return from above.
He tried to tell us how important it is to do His Father's will;

You may be asked to give your life up, that, in the end, you'll be living still.

> *He had to die, the choice was His,*
> *He chose to die, that we might live.*
> *He always forsook Himself, He did His Father's will,*
> *And in my heart, I know—my Lord is living still.*

APRIL '88

In April 1988, my daughter Erin, who was nine years old at the time, was about to take off on her bike WITHOUT the training wheels. We lived on a cul-de-sac, so traffic was not a problem. Off she went swerving and wobbling! Eventually, success. Always, there was someone watching and running alongside her as a protector, just like our Savior Jesus. April 1988 song: "A Savior Close At Hand."

"A Savior Close At Hand"

Remember when you first learned to walk,
how you stumbled around, fell to the ground?
Remember when you rode your first bike,
how you swerved around trees, skinned up your knees?

There was always a Savior close at hand,
Someone to dry your tears, to drive away your fears.
There was always a Savior close at hand,
Someone to lend a hand, someone to understand,
Someone to be your friend.

So remember, as you're living for the Lord,
you might stumble around, fall to the ground,
Jesus is your strength and guiding light.
He will guide you through the night,
fill your eyes with blessed sight.

There is always a Savior close at hand,
Someone to dry your tears, to drive away your fears.
There is always a Savior close at hand,
Someone to lend a hand, someone to understand,
Someone to be your friend.

Jesus will always be your friend;
He is your Savior close at hand.

MAY '88

I have had the opportunity to go to Ontario, Canada, and hike the Bruce Trail. This is a 30-mile trail at the top of the Bruce Peninsula. This trail follows an escarpment, the same escarpment that is Niagara Falls. There are places where you hike 200 feet above Georgian Bay, and a slip off the edge could plunge you into 45-degree water, and with a 50-pound backpack on you would sink like a rock. I thank Jesus that He always guided me along the shorelines on hiking trips and in life as well. May 1988 song.... "The One Whose Hand Sustains Me"

"The One Whose Hand Sustains Me"

As I walk along this shoreline and life's troubles fall and rise,
You're a friend who is my lifeline; Your voice can calm the raging tide.
You set my feet upon the dry ground, guide me through the rocky shore,
You're the one whose hand sustains me, sustains me evermore.

> *You are my Rock, You are my Ark, You are my Shelter in the storm,*
> *You are my Lord; You are the one who keeps me warm.*
> *You are the one who fills my thirst; in my heart, You shall be first.*
> *You are the one whose hand sustains me on and on.*

Though life may have its trials and the world be filled with strife
And decisions overwhelm me, so much darkness—where's the light?
Yet it's through this time of testing that I need to trust You more,
For You're the one whose hand sustains me, sustains me evermore.

> *You are my Rock, You are my Ark, You are my Shelter in the storm,*
> *You are my Lord; You are the one who keeps me warm.*
> *You are the one who fills my thirst; in my heart, You shall be first.*
> *You are the one whose hand sustains me on and on.*

And I thank You, Lord, for Your promise to always be there.
And I love You, Lord, for the time you've taken to care.

> *You are my Rock, You are my Ark, you are my Shelter in the storm,*
> *You are my Lord; You are the one who keeps me warm.*
> *You are the one who fills my thirst; in my heart, You shall be first.*
> *You are the one whose hand sustains me more and more,*
> *You are the one whose love sustains me—evermore.*

John M. Reichert

JUNE '88

On the way back from Canada to the United States, after a beautiful hike on the Bruce Trail, God gave me this non-Christian song: "Oh, Tobermory."

"Oh, Tobermory"

Home of the porcupine, the wolf, and the moose,
Atop the escarpment, out on the Bruce,
Walking to heaven along Georgian Bay,
I may return home, but my heart always stays.

> *Oh, Tobermory, you sound like a symphony,*
> *You are convincing me to see you again.*
> *Your seabirds are calling me, coastlines are begging me—*
> *Oh, Tobermory, to see you again.*

Hiking through heaven, out on the Bruce,
The elk and the porcupine, bear and the moose,
At night by the campfire, I heard someone say,
"I'll visit Ontario, another fine day."

> *Oh, Tobermory, you sound like a symphony,*
> *You are convincing me to see you again.*
> *Your seabirds are calling me, coastlines are begging me—*
> *Oh, Tobermory, I'll see you again.*

JULY '88

The next one I scribed down was in July 1988: "Jesus Is Coming Again." This became the first of the three songs I used to perform in a medley. August 1988…"I Will Be Like Him" and September 1988…"The Kingdom Is Coming."

"Jesus Is Coming Again"

Take comfort in the words I sing to You
That you may comfort another as brethren do.
Sorrow not for those who are dead, grieve not for those who sleep,
For someday, the Shepherd will come and gather His sheep.

> *Jesus is coming again, Jesus is coming again,*
> *With the trumpet of God sounding out loud,*
> *Calling His children to Him,*
> *Jesus is coming again.*

For the earth and the sea shall give up their dead;
The living—they will precede the Savior to wed,
And if we hold this truth, that Christ rose from the grave,
What a great reunion we'll have one glorious day!

> *Jesus is coming again, Jesus is coming again*
> *With the trumpet of God sounding out loud,*
> *Calling His children to Him,*
> *Jesus is coming again,*

Jesus is coming again,
Jesus is coming again.

AUGUST '88

"Beloved, now are we the children of God, and it doth not yet appear what we shall be, but we know that, when He shall appear, we shall be like Him; for we shall see Him as He is."

— 1 John 3:2 (KJV)

"I Will Be Like Him"

I will be like Him, perfect in every way, no sin.
Yes, I will be like Him when my Savior comes again.

> Transformed, in the twinkling of an eye.
> Reformed, when I meet Him in the sky.
> From mortal to immortal, in the kingdom, I will be,
> And all because God gave His Son to die in place of me.

I will be like Him, perfect in every way, no sin.
Yes, I will be like Him when my Savior comes again.

> O' Death, where is your victory?
> You've lost the fight for eternity.
> Christ Jesus, Messiah, has broken the power of sin,
> And when He comes to earth again, I will be like Him.

John M. Reichert

I will be like Him, perfect in every way, no sin.
Yes, I will be like Him when my Savior comes again.
When Jesus comes again.

SEPTEMBER '88

"The Kingdom Is Coming"

I know the kingdom is coming, I know the Lord's on His way.
I know the kingdom is coming. Oh, what a glorious day!
When there will be no more sorrow, when there will be no more pain,
I know the kingdom is coming, and Jesus Christ will reign.

> *Holy, Holy, Holy is the Lord,*
> *Holy, Holy, Holy is the Lord. Jesus is Lord.*

I know the kingdom is coming, I know the Lord's on His way.
I know the kingdom is coming; pray for that glorious day
When we will all join together and we will all live as one,
Praising God, the Father, and worshiping Jesus, the Son.

> *Holy, Holy, Holy is the Lord.*
> *Holy, Holy, Holy is the Lord.*
> *Holy, Holy, Holy is the Lord.*
> *Holy, Holy, Holy is the Lord.*
> *Jesus is Lord.*
> *Jesus is Lord.*
> *Jesus is Lord.*

John M. Reichert

In September 1988, Timberland Bible Church, South Bend, Indiana, asked me if I could write a song for their church—not as a "theme" song but just to kind of describe what the belief of the church was. As the month rolled by, I was wondering if this was going to happen in September—or maybe October. On the 28th of September, God gave me this song, and I could barely write it down fast enough. September 1988 song... "Children of God."

"Children of God"

Our God, the one and only God
Loved the world as one, gave His only Son
To Die, that we might live forever
Because of Jesus Christ, the Sacrifice, we are...

> *Children of God, let us praise the Father's name, for we are*
> *Children of God, let us fall upon our faces.*
> *He has blessed us with His spirit;*
> *If we hear and draw Him near us,*
> *He'll keep us children of God, children of God.*

Christ showed the way through His obedience;
The Father willed, Christ's blood was spilled
In death, He glorified His Father,
He suffered so; He was made whole; now we are...

> *Children of God, let us praise the Father's name, for we are*
> *Children of God, let us fall upon our faces.*
> *He has blessed us with His spirit;*

If we hear and draw Him near us,
He'll keep us children of God, Children of God.

All have sinned and come short of God's glory,
And death is the result of sin.
But God's gift is life, through His Son Jesus Christ
Repent and ask Jesus new life to begin.

Believe, be baptized with the spirit,
Wash away your sins, your soul be cleansed,
Saved by faith and not by works;
As Abraham became God's friend, we will be…

Children of God, let us praise the Father's name, for we are
Children of God, let us fall upon our faces.
He has blessed us with His spirit;
If we hear and draw Him near us.
He'll keep us children of God, Children of God.

John M. Reichert

OCTOBER '88

It's late 1988, and I have taken a job in sales with Glaxo Pharmaceutical. This meant many hours of driving from doctor's offices to pharmacies and to hospitals. This was a great time to listen to talk radio and as many Christian stations as I could—not the music part, as I did not want it to influence my writing. One of my favorite programs at that time was "Focus on the Family" with Dr. James Dobson. Prayer was the topic on one day, and the October 1988 song came out of that broadcast… "To Move God's Hands."

"To Move God's Hands"

A little girl lies dying in the hospital tonight,
Her little brother bends a knee and says a prayer by her bedside,
"God, You know I've teased her, You know I've pulled her hair,
But please send one more miracle, cause, God, You know I care."

A lonely woman lies awake in tears, her husband's gone again,
He says that he'll be working late, but she knows it's just pretend,
"God, You know I love him, and I want to be his friend,
But my strength is not enough alone; I need Your helping hand."

> *To move God's hands, say a faithful little prayer,*
> *To move God's hands, all your burdens He will bear.*
> *If you feel the load is much too great,*

> *And you feel you're sinking from the weight,*
> *Say a faithful little prayer, and God's hands will meet you there.*

A preacher sits alone in his study, his head is resting in his hands,
He wants the church to be more active, but he doesn't have a plan,
"God, move them with Your Spirit and fill them with desire,
Make their service hot for You; God, fill them with Your fire."

> *To move God's hands, say a faithful little prayer,*
> *To move God's hands, all your burdens He will bear.*
> *If you feel the load is much too great,*
> *And you feel you're sinking from the weight,*
> *Say a faithful little prayer, and God's hands will meet you there.*

John M. Reichert

NOVEMBER '88

Here's a little Christmas tune that came in November 1988: "A Gift for You."

"A Gift for You"

I want to give a gift to You, I want to give a gift to You,
I want to give a gift to You; my song is my gift for You.

I want to give a gift to You, I want to give a gift to You,
I want to give a gift to You; my love is my gift for You.

I want to give a gift to You, I want to give a gift to You,
I want to give a gift to You; my life is my gift for You.

> *I want to give something back to You*
> *Cause you gave something special to me.*
> *Your Son, who will soon come to rule the world,*
> *Is the greatest gift I could ever receive.*

I want to give a gift to You, I want to give a gift to You,
I want to give a gift to You; My ALL is my gift for You.
My ALL is my gift for You; My ALL is my gift for You.

I don't know about you, but I like to get presents at Christmas. Better than that, I like to give presents—not just at Christmas but at any time of year. The greatest gift of all is to invite Jesus into your heart as your personal Savior. The greatest gift to have ever been given!

"I Think Every Day Should Be Just Like Christmas"

Can you tell me why we celebrate Christmas?
Is it because of all the presents we get?
Is it because of all the turkey and dressing?
Can you tell me why so many forget?

Can you tell me why we celebrate Christmas?
To put a smile on the face of a child?
Is it just an excuse for a party
where everyone's emotions run wild?

> *Christmas is the day when the Christ child was born,*
> *The greatest gift that ever was given.*
> *And when His service was through,*
> *He died for the world,*
> *That the world's sin might be forgiven,*
> *That the world's sin might be forgiven.*

Can you tell me why we celebrate Christmas
in December on one single day?
I think every day should be just like Christmas,
and I think that God would want it that way.

> *For today in the world, someone will open God's gift*
> *And take Jesus as their only Savior.*

John M. Reichert

Any time of the day, any day of the year,
Talk to God, and Christmas will appear;
Talk to God, and Christmas will appear

because Christmas is the day that the Christ child was born,
The greatest gift that ever was given.
And when His service was through, He died for the world,
That the whole world might be forgiven.
I think every day should be just like Christmas.

JANUARY '89

There were no songs given to me in December 1988, but January 1989 started with a rocker called "Judas." At the time, my six-year-old son Zachary would run in circles when I would rehearse this song and sing the lyric "Jewish" instead of "Judas." It was hysterical. January 1989 song ... "Judas."

"Judas"

"Judas, Judas," I can still hear Peter say,
"Judas, Judas, what are you doing? That's the Lord you chose to betray."

"Did you know, when you were born,
that you would be a chosen one?
To fulfill His holy word
and be the one to kiss God's Son?"

"Judas, Judas," I can still hear Peter say,
"Judas, Judas, what are you doing? That's the Lord you chose to betray."

"You have walked with the Lord,
and you have carried His holy sword,
But your life was just a lie,
and for this, you hung and died."

"Judas, Judas," I can still hear Peter say,
"Judas, Judas, what are you doing? That's the Lord you chose to
 betray."

Two thousand years have come and gone.
Still, Peter sings the same old song,
You still betray Him, you use no kiss;
it's in your words and the way you live.

"Judas, you're a Judas," I can still hear Peter say,
"Judas, you're a Judas, what are you doing? That's the Lord you
 chose to betray.
What are you doing? That's the Lord you chose to betray."

James 4:13–15 (KJV) tells us, "Come now ye that say today or tomorrow we will go into such a city and continue there a year and buy and sell and get gain; whereas ye know not what shall be on the morrow. For what is your life? It is even a vapor that appeareth for a little time and then vanishes away. For ye ought to say, If the Lord will, we shall live, and do this or that."

As on a cold frosty morning, when you breathe out a vapor and it quickly vanishes, so is our life in God's timeframe. January 1989: "Lead Me, Guide Me."

"Lead Me, Guide Me"

Lead me, guide me, show me, Lord, the way;
Spirit, speak to my soul, help me day to day.
For life is just a fleeting breath that's gone before Your face,
Lead me, guide me, to Your Holy Place.

Keep me, warm me, in Your tender arms,
With Your hand, sustain me, keep me from all harm.
And if my faith should show some doubt, just tighten Your embrace;
Keep me, warm me, in Your loving grace.

> *You love me, care for me every single day,*
> *You gave Your life to die, the one and only way.*

Teach me, help me, more like You to be,
Help me to deny myself, set my sight on Thee
That someday I may kneel before and hear my Savior say,
"Well done, faithful, enter through My gate."

> *You love me, care for me every single day,*
> *You gave Your life to die, the one and only way.*

Teach me, help me, more like You to be,
Help me to deny myself, set my sight on Thee
That someday I may kneel before and hear my Savior say,
"Well done, faithful, enter through My gate."

Sometimes I like to take a popular scripture, like Psalm 23, and then look at the scripture before it or the one after it. In this case, Psalm 24:1–10 was the inspiration for this third January 1989 song, "The King of Glory."

"The King of Glory"

The earth is the Lord's, yes, the earth is the Lord's, and all that she can hold;
The earth is the Lord's, yes, the earth is the Lord's, and all that she can hold.

> Who is this King of Glory? The Lord Almighty and True;
> Who is this King of Glory? The Lord Almighty and True.

Who will ascend to the Hill of the Lord and stand in His Holy Place?
He who has heart and hands pure and clean is the one to seek the King's Holy Face.

> Who is this King of Glory? The Lord Almighty and True;
> Who is this King of Glory? The Lord Almighty and True.

> So, lift up your heads all ye gates,
> Lift up your heads all ye doors,
> And the King of Glory will come in.

The earth is the Lord's, yes, the earth is the Lord's, and all that she can hold;
The earth is the Lord's, yes, the earth is the Lord's, and all that she can hold.
Who is this King of Glory? The Lord Almighty and True;
Who is this King of Glory? The Lord Almighty and True.

FEBRUARY '89

"Are You Ready?"

Are you ready? For the coming of the Lord?
Are you ready? To hear His final word?
Are you ready to face what awaits you at the end of the road
Are you ready for the coming, for the coming of the Lord?

Are you ready for the coming of the Lord?
For a life that holds no sorrows, a life that holds no war,
Have your sins all been forgiven, your faith and hope restored—
Are you ready for the coming, for the coming of the Lord?

Are you ready? For the coming of the Lord?
Are you ready? To hear His final word?
Are you ready to face what awaits you at the end of the road?
Are you ready for the coming, for the coming of the Lord?

Are you ready to give up everything you own?
Your house, your cars, your business, your jewelry made of stone?
And share more riches than any king could ever know—
Are you ready to live with Jesus and give up everything you own?

Are you ready? For the coming of the Lord?
Are you ready? To hear His final word?

John M. Reichert

> *Are you ready to face what awaits you at the end of the road?*
> *Are you ready for the coming, for the coming of the Lord?*

> *Are you ready? Are you ready?*
> *Are you ready for the coming of the Lord?*
> *Are you ready? Are you ready?*
> *Are you ready for the coming of the Lord?*

Are you ready to walk with Jesus side by side?
Are you ready to spend forever and in His love abide?
Have you set your sights on Glory and prayed His kingdom nigh?
Are you ready to walk with Jesus, with Jesus side by side?

> *Are you ready? For the coming of the Lord?*
> *Are you ready? To hear His final word?*
> *Are you ready to face what awaits you at the end of the road?*
> *Are you ready for the coming, for the coming of the Lord?*

MARCH '89

A friend of mine asked me how I knew I had Jesus in my heart. I told him it was simple; there is a peace and a comfort that, no matter what happens, it is going to be alright. March 1989 song… "That's How I Know."

"That's How I Know"

How do you know when Jesus is in your heart?
Do you see new beginnings, do you see a new start?
How do you feel when dark clouds roll over you?
Do you hide in the shadows or let the SON through?

> *Jesus is in my heart today;*
> *He drives the darkness all away.*
> *He brings me comfort and takes away my fears—*
> *That's how I know that He is near.*

Where do you go when the pain's much too great?
Who do you turn to, on whom do you wait?
Who do you know that can handle your every care?
Someone who is strong enough, your burdens to bear.

> *Jesus is in my heart today;*
> *He drives the darkness all away.*
> *He brings me comfort and takes away my fears—*
> *That's how I know that He is near.*

John M. Reichert

How can they say that there is no guiding hand?
It just seems to happen—there's no Master Plan.
They never knew, alongside, You walked with them,
They heard not Your whisper or plea to come in.

> *They never heard the Savior say, all your debts of sin I've paid,*
> *They never knew His death meant life for them and me.*
> *I guess you could say they've never seen,*
> *Once I was blind, but now, I see—Jesus lives inside of me.*
> *He brings me comfort, and He takes away my fears—*
> *That's how I know that He is near; that's how I know Jesus cares.*

APRIL '89

According to the legend, the dogwood felt great sorrow for the role it played in Jesus Christ's death. While on the cross, Jesus sensed the tree's anguish, and He decided to transform it so that it could never again be used in crucifixion. From that point on, the dogwood was no longer a tall, stately forest tree. Rather, it became a small and shrub-like tree with thin and twisted limbs. Jesus was taken down from the cross and placed in a tomb. Three days later, He arose from the dead. At the same time, the dogwoods in the forest burst into bloom, and they continue to do so right around Easter in what's believed to be a celebration of Jesus' resurrection. It's still said to carry the marks of Jesus' crucifixion. Its four large petals represent the cross He died upon, and each petal displays four red-tinged notches that are said to represent four nail holes. And in the center of each flower is a green cluster that is symbolic of Jesus' crown of thorns.

—Bower and Branch

"The Dogwood Song"

Is it truth or legend? Can history bear it out
That the dogwood once was mighty, the wood was strong and stout,
That the Romans used to use it for those they crucified,
A mastery of suffering, where the Savior hung and died?

> *"Thank you for sharing in the suffering of My Son,"*
> *Said God to the dogwood tree.*
> *"No more will man use you for this activity;*
> *You played your part to secure eternity,"*
> *Said God to the dogwood tree.*

"Your wood I will make twisted, no crosses will you make,
Except your lovely flower, a cross the petals shape,
On each, a rusty nail print encircled by His blood
To remind us of His agony and of His endless love."

> *"Thank you for sharing in the suffering of My Son,"*
> *Said God to the dogwood tree.*
> *"No more will man use you for this activity;*
> *You played your part to secure eternity,"*
> *Said God to the dogwood tree.*

> *"You bore my Son, you were with Him to the end,*
> *And I will make you a beautiful tree, for you are My friend."*

"In the center of your petals, I will place a crown of thorns
To remind us of the world's hate and of its thoughtless scorn,
That the dogwood be remembered, who bore the King of Kings,
A tree that knew so much death knew life eternally."

"Thank you for sharing in the suffering of My Son,"
Said God to the dogwood tree.
"No more will man use you for this activity;
You played your part to secure eternity,"
Said God to the dogwood tree.

For he shall give his angels charge over thee, to keep thee in all thy ways. They shall bear thee up in their hands, lest thou dash thy foot against a stone.

— Psalm 91:11–12 (KJV)

"Angels of the King"

In the stillness of the night,
I can always hear their ringing,
And to my soul, it brings delight,
the angels of the King as they are singing.

> *Hosanna, Hosanna, Name above every name*
> *Hosanna, Hosanna, Forever is Your reign.*

And every earthly ear should hark
to a sound that's oh, so thrilling,
As an angel with a harp that
speaks a Name that's oh, so filling.

> *Hosanna, Hosanna, Name above every name*
> *Hosanna, Hosanna, Forever is Your reign.*

John M. Reichert

Hosanna, Hosanna, Hosanna
Hosanna, Hosanna, Hosanna

When the King of Kings returns
and brings His choir of angels,
I know a place has been reserved
for me to sing forever His praises.

Hosanna, Hosanna, Name above every name
Hosanna, Hosanna, Forever is Your reign.

Hosanna, Hosanna, Name above every name
Hosanna, Hosanna, Forever is Your reign.

MAY '89

And thou shalt love the Lord thy God with all thine heart, and with all thy soul, and with all thy might.

— Deuteronomy 6:5 (KJV)

This is one of Steve's favorites! May 1989 Song… "Heart and Soul and Might."

"Heart and Soul and Might"

I know that You are the only one to give up Your only Son, for me.
I must say that I cannot repay all the love that You gave, for me.

> *So, I give myself to You, in heart and soul and might*
> *To be worthy of the service of the King.*
> *And I throw away the old and usher in the new,*
> *Laying all I have before the mighty King.*

I know that You will be using me to further Your ministry of love,
So, I leave my wealth, my cloak, and my sandals, Lord, to go out into the world for You.

> *So, I give myself to You, in heart and soul and might*
> *To be worthy of the service of the King.*
> *And I throw away the old and usher in the new,*
> *Laying all I have before the mighty King.*

*I know that You are the only One to give up Your only Son, for me,
For me, For me.*

JUNE '89

Paul, a follower of Jesus Christ, tells us in Ephesians 6:12 (KJV) that there is a battle going on in heavenly places, a spiritual battle for our souls. Ephesians 6:12 (KJV): "For we wrestle not against flesh and blood, but against principalities, against powers, against the rulers of the darkness of this world, against spiritual wickedness in high places."

I have experienced this personally. While on a family vacation in Bend, Oregon, my son Zachary and I took a short hike in the woods before dinner. While in the woods, we came upon a side trail that led to a structure made of branches and leaves. Zach so wanted to go explore the structure, but the hair on my neck was standing up—as if there was something evil nearby. I recommended we return to the hotel and prepare for dinner. That night, while asleep, I experienced my guardian angel standing over my bed and fighting evil spirits with a sword and shield. My angel is a tremendous warrior, and he fought all night until I awoke in the morning. I am so glad my angel was there.

"Invisible War"

There's a battle going on, a war unseen. A fight for all eternity,
A battle going on, the warriors are keen. They fight for the souls of you and me.

> *Invisible war, invisible war, powers fight principalities.*
> *Invisible war, invisible war,*
> *You will hear no gunshot; you will hear no cannon roar*
> *In the invisible, visible war.*

We must have a plan against a darker fate. And put on the armor of our God—
Truth and Righteousness, a shield of faith, with the Gospel of Peace, our feet, we shod.

> *Invisible war, invisible war, powers fight principalities.*
> *Invisible war, invisible war,*
> *You will hear no gunshot, you will hear no cannon roar*
> *In the invisible, visible war.*

> *Look around and see the damage done; the Destroyer preys on everyone;*
> *He ruins souls and lives every day.*
> *You can quench his fiery darts by hiding God's word in your heart*
> *And following the path that Jesus paved.*

Jesus showed the way with the spirit's sword when He was tested as a man;
We, too, must obey and know God's word and, against the devil, take a stand.

> *Invisible war, invisible war, powers fight principalities.*
> *Invisible war, invisible war,*
> *You will hear no gunshot, you will hear no cannon roar*
> *In the invisible, visible war.*
> *You will hear no gunshot, you will hear no cannon roar In the invisible, visible war.*

This song in June 1989 is as relevant today as when God gave it to me then. With CRT, transgenderism, and all the other sexuality being taught in our public schools, it is so vitally important that the Children be taught about Jesus continuously. Proverbs 22:6 (KJV) tells us, "Train up a child in the way he should go: and when he is old, he will not depart from it." The devil knows this verse too. June 1989 song… "Children Need Jesus Too."

"Children Need Jesus Too"

Do you wonder who's rocking the cradle while moms and dads work all day?
Do you wonder if they're being told fables, is the life of Christ being displayed?
Do you wonder, should the church provide daycare, should the government set the rules?
Parents, please teach Jesus to your children 'cause children need Jesus too.

> *They've taken Christ out of our Christmas,*
> *They've taken Christ out of our schools.*
> *Parents, please teach Jesus to our children*
> *'Cause children need Jesus too.*
>
> *Teach them when you lie down, teach them when you rise,*
> *Teach them when you're walking along the roadside.*
> *Paint it on your doorpost for the world to see*
> *That Jesus dwells within the hearts of you and me.*

Because the children we are teaching today will be the teachers teaching tomorrow.
May they lead God's family back to the way and avoid the path of pain and sorrow,
May they hold onto the training and hold on to the truth,
May they let the love of Jesus shine through,
And be parents who teach Jesus to their children because they know children need Jesus too.

> *And help put Christ back into our Christmas,*
> *And help put Christ back into our schools,*
> *And be parents who teach Jesus to their children*
> *'Cause children need Jesus too.*

JULY '89

I have always enjoyed the passage in Isaiah, chapter 40, verse 31 (KJV): "they that wait upon the Lord shall renew their strength; they shall mount up with wings as eagles; they shall run, and not be weary; and they shall walk, and not faint." I have recited this verse in my heart many times when climbing a steep switchback in the mountains. July 1989 song "He Is the King."

"He Is the King"

Have you not heard, have you not seen, that the one who divided the bread He calmed the sea
He will not slumber; He will not sleep. He is always there to help you in time of need.

> *Have you not heard, have you not seen*
> *He is a Rock; He is a Refuge in time of need.*
> *He'll help you fly like an eagle on the wing;*
> *He is a Rock, He is a Refuge, He is the King.*

If you feel down, if you feel weak, He'll wrap His loving arms around and give you strength;
He knows your prayers, your every call, and He has already provided for them all.

Have you not heard, have you not seen
He is a Rock; He is a Refuge in time of need.
He'll help you fly like an eagle on the wing;
He is a Rock, He is a Refuge, He is the King.

Praise His name, Praise His name,
Sing with the heavenly beings
And proclaim Him, King of Kings.

If you feel lonely, if you feel lost, if you feel like one of the disciples on a sea that's tossed,
One little word will bring forth peace, for even the wildest of tempests still believe.

Have you not heard, have you not seen
He is a Rock; He is a Refuge in time of need.
He'll help you fly like an eagle on the wing;
He is a Rock, He is a Refuge, He is the King.

AUGUST '89

You have heard of Christmas in July; I must have been thinking about snow in August. August 1989 song… "Life Is Like a Snowflake." Each one of us is unique. Find the purpose God has for you and fulfill it.

"Life Is Like a Snowflake"

God created every snowflake, different from the rest,
Some are big, and some are small, but each one is equally blessed,
Some make mighty fortresses that sit on mountains high,
Some don't stay around so long; it seems too soon they die.
Some make little children laugh when they touch them on the nose,
Some just fly off with the wind; no one knows just where they go.

> *Life is like a snowflake; each one is unique.*
> *Each one holds a purpose, and that is what we seek—*
> *To serve the King of Ages and do the best we can,*
> *For life is like a snowflake that falls from the Master's Hand.*

But snowflakes come from water, and to water, they return,
Like man who comes from earthy dust, a lesson to be learned
That the time that God has given us is shorter than we know,
So, serve the King with all of your might, with all your heart and soul.

John M. Reichert

Life is like a snowflake; each one is unique.
Each one holds a purpose, and that is what we seek—
To serve the King of Ages and do the best we can,
For life is like a snowflake that falls from the Master's Hand,

Life is like a snowflake that falls from the Master's Hand.

SEPTEMBER '89

I played high school basketball at a small school. I was on the varsity in my junior and senior years. As players, we were required to wear cream-colored pants with a shirt and tie and a blazer. Usually, a blue blazer as our colors were blue and gold. Most of us chose chords as our trousers of choice. As the b-team game starts in the third quarter, the varsity team would rise and make their way to the locker room to dress for the game. After a game one evening, a lady who I did not know came up to me and asked me where I got my chords. Puzzled, I told her which store they were purchased at, but curiously I asked why she wanted to know. She told me that her fourth-grade son watched everything I did all the time. Also, he wanted to dress exactly like me. What an awakening. Somebody somewhere is always watching what you do and listening to what you say. Can they see Jesus in you? September 1989 song… "Can They See Jesus?"

"Can They See Jesus?"

Can they see Jesus in you? Can they see Jesus in you?
Can they hear His truth in what you say, see His love in all you do?
Can they see Jesus in you?

I have heard we're all just actors and the world is just a stage,
And as the script unfolds to reveal the role of the character you play,
Are you aware of those who watch you and hang on every word you say?
Is your reflection of the Son of love in your living day by day?

> *Can they see Jesus in you? Can they see Jesus in you?*
> *Can they hear His truth in what you say, see His love in all you do?*
> *Can they see Jesus in you?*

We're all children of the Father; He shared His only Son with you,
And it would be neglect if you forget to share with someone too.
The secret of the mystery of how Jesus lives in you,
And could you bear the pain to hear the names of those who saw no King in you?

> *Can they see Jesus in you? Can they see Jesus in you?*
> *Can they hear His truth in what you say, see His love in all you do?*
> *Can they see Jesus in you?*

OCTOBER '89

In October 1989, God had me scribe lyrics for a song "Pipe Dream." However, it was one of those things where no music was ever put with these lyrics. When writing, sometimes the music comes first, and the lyrics are fit to the music. Sometimes the lyrics are first, and the music comes later. In a good majority of the songs, the two happen together.

I really don't even remember what inspired these lyrics, but I like them… "Pipe Dream."

"Pipe Dream"

You've finally graduated, and you're thinking that you're cool,
You're working at a new job now, you're finally out of school,
You're thinking life's so easy, you're thinking it's a breeze,
Well, let me tell you this, son, you are living in a dream. A Pipe Dream.

You say you've got a lady, and this one's going to last,
You say there'll be no fighting like there had been in the past,
You say she makes you happy, she makes you want to scream,
Well, let me tell you this, son, you might be living in a dream. A Pipe Dream,

> *You are living in a Pipe Dream, living in a Pipe Dream,*
> *The layers are separating, and you think you'll be the cream,*

Well, let me tell you this, son, you're probably living in a dream. A Pipe Dream.

You've finally found a Savior, the devil's been pushed aside,
You think he'll cause you no more trouble, you've got the gift of eternal life,
He preys upon the proud son, so don't you be deceived,
There'll still be trials and temptations if you're living in a dream. A Pipe Dream.

You are living in a Pipe Dream, living in a Pipe Dream,
The layers are separating, and you think you'll be the cream,
Well, let me tell you this, son, you're probably living in a dream. A Pipe Dream.

NOVEMBER '89

November 1989 brought an instrumental called "Flight of the Wisemen."

DECEMBER '89

December was not a Christmas song month this year. A friend of mine was going through a tough relational season, and this was penned to hopefully help them feel a bit better.

"Creator of the Heart"

It must be great, the pain that you feel from your broken heart.
Don't you know that He loves you?
Don't you know that He's cared for you right from the start?

It must be hard, keeping a smile while things are falling apart,
Still, I know that He loves you;
Still, I know that He's cared for you right from the start.

> *He loves you—more than you may ever know,*
> *He loves you—more than I can say,*
> *He loves you—more than anyone can show,*
> *He provides the seasons, Keeper of the reasons, Maker, Creator of the Heart.*

Everything's set—it runs on His time—I know it must be hard to wait,
Still, He's walking beside you;
Still, He offers His hand if you'll reach out and take.

> *He loves you—more than you may ever know,*
> *He loves you—more than I can say,*
> *He loves you—more than anyone can show,*
> *He provides the seasons, Keeper of the reasons, Maker, Creator of the Heart.*
>
> *He knows what suffering is all about, He gave His Son up to die,*
> *He holds the future—there is no doubt, He's offering a better life.*
> *And though the answers seem hard to find, you must keep the faith;*
> *He gave His Son, a guiding light, to guide you on the narrow way.*

If you hang on, it will all work out, though the end is hard to see,
Still, His promise is love for you;
Still, His promises last for eternity.

> *He loves you—more than you may ever know,*
> *He loves you—more than I can say,*
> *He loves you—more than anyone can show,*
> *He provides the seasons, Keeper of the reasons,*
> *Maker, Creator of the Heart.*

John M. Reichert

JANUARY '90

Galatians 6:2 (KJV) states, "Bear ye one another's burdens, and so fulfill the law of Christ."

This verse was part of a Bible study I was having at that time. The Bible study brought to memory the backpacking trip in Montana the previous year. I came down with a terrible GI problem with six miles to go of a thirty-mile trip. My friend, Jim "Bubba" Harmeson, carried my backpack and his backpack the last six miles. He carried me.

"Carry"

Isn't that the way it always seems to go?
When you get down, you're down so low.
Isn't that the way it always seems to be?
Nobody 'round you when you're down on your knees.

I don't know if this is wrong or right,
Asking God to make your burden light.
I don't know if this is what I should do,
Asking God to let me carry it too.

> *I want to carry, I want to carry,*
> *I want to shoulder your load,*
> *help you back on the road,*
> *I want to carry, carry your load.*

Maybe this will help you, brother, maybe not;
our God is faithful where the world is not.
Maybe I'll fulfill another Christian law;
maybe I've done nothing, nothing at all.

My Bible tells me God will carry me through,
I know He's strong enough to carry you too.
If we walk this road as one, not two,
We'll hear Him calling through.

> *I want to carry, I want to carry,*
> *I want to shoulder your load,*
> *help you back on the road,*
> *I want to carry, carry your load.*
>
> *I want to carry, I want to carry,*
> *I want to shoulder your load,*
> *help you back on the road,*
> *I want to carry, carry your load.*

John M. Reichert

FEBRUARY '90

The church I was attending in February 1990 was looking for Sunday school teachers and helpers. They stated that they had all these kids for classes but no one to teach them. This is one of my all-time favorites, and it has a neat chord progression that you obviously can't hear.

"Who Will Be There"

Empty classrooms—Oh, what a shame,
No one to teach them or call out their names.
Empty chalkboards, no lessons to learn,
A room full of children yearning to learn.

> *Who will be their guiding light? Who will show them wrong from right?*
> *Who'll open their hearts to the word?*
> *Who will start them on their way of loving Jesus day by day?*
> *Who'll open their hearts to the Lord?*

> *Who will be there? Who will be there?*
> *Who will be there for the children today?*
> *Who will be there? Who will be there?*
> *Who will be there to teach the children today?*

Suffer the children, come let them see,
They can inherit the kingdom with you and me.
But they will need teachers, oh, who will it be?
To plant in the children the seeds that they need.

> *Who will be their guiding light? Who will show them wrong from right?*
> *Who'll open their hearts to the word?*
> *Who will start them on their way of loving Jesus day by day?*
> *Who'll open their hearts to the Lord?*
>
> *Who will be there? Who will be there?*
> *Who will be there for the children today?*
> *Who will be there? Who will be there?*
> *Who will be there to teach the children today?*

John M. Reichert

MARCH '90

My friend Steve, who plays bass, and I were invited to sing for a "ladies' night" banquet. These were not the ladies from our church but from another church in town. These are always fun to do because we also get to partake of the wonderful meal, usually a carry-in. One of the songs we sang at the banquet was March 1990 song "All My Days." One of the ladies came up to me after the service and said to me, "It's about time we have a Christian John Denver…" I just laughed! I should have said, "Far out!" The song did have kind of a JD sound. What a great compliment.

"All My Days"

All my days have been set for me,
All my days come from above,
All my days are being kept for me,
All my days, I need Your love.

Lord, Your ways—they are unknown to me,
Lord, Your ways—I'll never understand,
Lord, Your ways—they are a mystery,
So all my days I'll hold Your hand.

Lord, I'll follow where You lead,
Through every valley, dark with fear.

Lord, stay close enough so every little whisper
I can hear.

All my days, I'll spend worshiping,
All my days, I will be true to You,
All my days, I'll be exalting,
All my days, I'm loving You.

Lord, I'll follow where You lead,
Through every valley, dark with fear.
Lord, stay close enough so every little whisper
I can hear.

All my days have been set for me;
all my days come from above,
All my days are being kept for me;
All my days, I need Your love.

John M. Reichert

MAY '90

No April 1990 song. The song in my heart in April 1990 was my son Luke being born! Luke continues to be a blessing as an adult man. He has a degree in Chemical Engineering with a minor in Finance and is working on an MBA at Indiana University while working full-time.

I'm a Vince Gill fan. I like the style of music he writes. He is a phenomenal guitar player. But what I like most is his high vocal range. This song that God gave me was written in my high range when I was much younger. This is probably my friend Steve's all-time favorite, and whenever we are together, he always says, "Let's do 'Morning Star.'"

"Morning Star"

Sometimes dark clouds follow me around,
They do their best to bring me down.
That's when I say a prayer; I say it right out loud,
O Lord, please turn this day around... Then that

> *Morning star rises in my heart,*
> *And I see, O yes, I see that the*
> *Morning star that rises in my heart,*
> *It is there to set the captive free.*

Sometimes I get tired, I just get tired of trying,
Sometimes I feel so discouraged.
In these times, it's so hard to talk about Christ's dying;
In these times, it takes so much courage... Then that

> Morning star rises in my heart,
> And I see, O yes, I see that the
> Morning Star that rises in my heart,
> It is there to set the captive free.

Sometimes I need reminded that on this kingdom road,
Stormy days will come, and they will go.
Sometimes I need reminded of the promise of my Lord,
That I will never, ever be alone... Then that

> Morning star rises in my heart,
> And I see, O yes, I see that the
> Morning star that rises in my heart,
> It is there to set the captive free.

Looks like it's going to be another rainy day,
Looks like another day I need to pray.

> Morning star, rise up in my heart,
> Let me see, O let me see that the
> Morning star that rises in my heart,
> It is there to set the captive free.

John M. Reichert

MAY '90

And they sing the Song of Moses the servant of God, and the song of the Lamb, saying, Great and marvelous are thy works, Lord God Almighty; Just and true are thy ways, thou King of saints.

— Revelation 15:3–4 (KJV)

"Song of Moses"

Great and marvelous Your deeds,
Lord God almighty.
Great and marvelous Your deeds,
Lord God almighty,
Lord God almighty.

> *Who will not fear You, O Lord,*
> *And bring honor to Your name?*
> *Who will not fear You, O Lord,*
> *And bring honor to Your name?*

Great and marvelous Your deeds,
Lord God almighty.
Great and marvelous Your deeds,
Lord God almighty,

Lord God almighty.

> *For You alone are Holy,*
> *For You alone are true.*
> *For You alone are Holy, For You alone are true.*

Great and marvelous Your deeds,
Lord God almighty.
Great and marvelous Your deeds,
Lord God almighty,
Lord God almighty.

> *All nations will come and worship before You,*
> *For Your righteous acts have been revealed.*
> *All nations will come and worship before You,*
> *For Your righteous acts have been revealed.*

Great and marvelous Your deeds,
Lord God almighty.
Great and marvelous Your deeds,
Lord God almighty, Lord God almighty.

John M. Reichert

JUNE '90

Usually, in July, I do a backpacking trip to the mountains. Many times, I start organizing and packing while there is still snow on the ground. While I'm up high on a mountainside, I just feel closer to God.

June 1990, God let me scribe down another mountain song. As far as I can see from that mountainside, God's love for me is farther than that!!!

"That's How Much"

Higher than the mountains, deeper than the sea—
That's how much He loves me, my Jesus, He loves me.
He reaches farther than the farthest place a man could ever be,
For that's how much He loves me, my Jesus, He loves me

> *And I will sing that Jesus loves me,*
> *I will sing that Jesus cares.*
> *Oh, it doesn't matter where I am or where I plan to be—*
> *That's how much He loves me, my Jesus, He loves me.*

To walk the way of suffering, to give His life for me,
To ask forgiveness for the world while hanging on the tree.
Forsaken by His Father in His greatest time of need,
He expressed the greatest love, expressed His love for me.

And I will sing that Jesus loves me,
I will sing that Jesus cares.
Oh, it doesn't matter where I am or where I plan to be—
That's how much He loves me, my Jesus, He loves me.

And I will sing that Jesus loves me,
I will sing that Jesus cares.
Oh, it doesn't matter where I am or where I plan to be—
That's how much He loves me, my Jesus, He loves me.

JULY '90

Picking a favorite song is like choosing which child is your favorite. This favorite child came in July of 1990. It is self-explanatory. Jesus said in John 7:37 (KJV): "If any man thirst, let him come unto me and drink…"

"O Galilean"

There was a man who could not see,
He was blind from birth.
He met the man from Galilee
Who helped him see his worth.

There was a child who could not walk,
Those legs were bent and torn.
He heard the Galilean talk,
And he could run once more.

> *O, Galilean, You heal the hurt,*
> *Take away the pain.*
> *You are the drink to those who thirst;*
> *You make them whole again.*

There was a woman seeking rest,
Faith drew her to Him.
And as the Galilean passed,
She reached and touched His hem.

> O, Galilean, You heal the hurt,
> Take away the pain.
> You are the drink to those who thirst;
> You make them whole again.

I came to thee, O, Galilean,
So imperfect too.
It was my sin so deep within
That broke my heart into.

> O, Galilean, You healed my heart
> And took away my pain.
> You sewed the rent from piercing dark
> and made me whole again.

> O, Galilean, You heal the hurt,
> Take away the pain.
> You are the drink to those who thirst;
> you make them whole again.

John M. Reichert

SEPTEMBER '90

God gave me a set of lyrics but no music for this one. September 1990 song… "The Priest Lives On."

"The Priest Lives On"

Before the alter, he lays the sins down,
He sacrifices where no blemish is found.
And if before his God his favor is found,
the priest lives on.

The line of Aaron, the tribe of Levi,
The chosen one to stand before their God and cry,
"Forgive us, Father, for the sins that we've done."
And let the priest live on.

> *The priest lives on to be my intercessor,*
> *He stands before the throne, my true confessor.*
> *I thank the Most High God He heard his song*
> *And let the priest live on.*

The children yearly would gather around,
Before the temple, they'd wait to hear the sound.
And if they heard the bells upon his gown,
they knew the priest lives on.

> *The priest lives on to be my intercessor*
> *He stands before the throne my true confessor*
> *I thank the Most High God He heard his song*
> *And let the priest live on*

There comes another who is different from these,
Not of the bloodline or genealogy.
He is the chosen One, God's only Son;
A priest to live on.

No yearly sacrifice now needs to be made:
One death, One sacrifice, the Priest in the grave.
And on the third day, God called out His Son,
And the priest lives on.

> *The priest lives on to be my intercessor,*
> *He stands before the throne, my true confessor.*
> *I thank the Most High God He raised His Son*
> *so that the priest lives on.*

You can't beat the Bible story when Peter saw Jesus walking on water. Peter had seen other miracles and, of course, wanted to walk on water too. But when he got out there and it got real, Peter took his eye off Jesus, and he was now caught in the middle of a miracle. Have you ever been caught in a miracle?

"Middle of a Miracle"

Out on the horizon, a figure appears,
First to recognize Him as the man draws near,
Do my eyes deceive me, coming straightway from shore.
Walking on the water, the One we call Lord?

If it's really You, Lord, won't You call out my name?
"Peter, come and join Me and walk just the same."
When I felt the wind, when I saw the waves,
I took my eyes from Jesus, and my faith began to fade.

> I'm caught in the middle of a miracle,
> Caught in something I don't really understand,
> Caught in the middle of a miracle,
> Will my faith hold true? Will His love see me through
> This miracle?

When you walk with Jesus, you're stepping out in faith,
You leave the boat behind—it's the risk that you must take.
If you feel you're sinking, just look into His eyes,
His hands are reaching for you, yes, He will help you rise.

> And you're caught in the middle of a miracle,
> Caught in something you don't really understand,
> Caught in the middle of a miracle,
> Will your faith hold true? Will His love see you through
> This miracle?

> And if you keep your eyes on Jesus,
> He will never ever let you down.
> Just keep your eyes fixed on Jesus,
> Fixed upon the solid ground.

Because out on the horizon, a kingdom appears,
For those who trust His guidance and draw the Lord near.
It's nothing you can work for; it depends upon your faith,
Provided for by Jesus and God's saving grace.

> *So be caught in the middle of a miracle,*
> *Caught in something you will someday understand,*
> *Caught in the middle of a miracle,*
> *Where your faith will hold true, and His love sees you through This miracle.*

When you get up high on the alpine slopes, you will find some of the most amazing, intricate little plants with the most delicate purple flowers, thriving in a very windy harsh environment. Around these flowers flutter the most beautiful, tiny, black and kingly blue butterflies I have ever seen. I have spent many days sitting there watching them and wondering how someone could say there is no God.

"Mountains of Montana"

Do You ever dwell in these purple mountain majesty,
Lofty spires, my heart inquires, of Thee.
When I dare to climb to Thee, a humbling spirit drives me to my knees,
I look to find, among the pines, I see,

> *Even in the Mountains of Montana, God will be there,*
> *Even in the hollow of the canyons, my God will care.*

> *There is not a place that He cannot be; He'll meet you anywhere;*
> *Even in the mountains of Montana, God is there.*

I see Your face in the river cold that flows down from the mountain snows,
I feel Your grace upon my face when the sun shows.
I feel Your breath as the wind runs by; I see Your depth in the mountain sky.
Your spirit sings from eagles' wings as she flies.

> *Even in the Mountains of Montana, God will be there,*
> *Even in the hollow of the canyons, my God will care.*
> *There is not a place that He cannot be; He'll meet you anywhere;*
> *Even in the mountains of Montana, God is there.*
> *Even in the Mountains of Montana, God is there.*

A favorite psalm of mine, sometimes known as the traveler's psalm, is Psalm 121. I fell in love with this passage after the high school choir (1972) performed this song. I wish I could remember the composer and title, but I can't. What I remember is that it was based around this biblical text. Psalm 121:1–8 (KJV), "I will lift up mine eyes unto the hills. From whence cometh my help? My help cometh from the Lord who made heaven and earth. He will not suffer thy foot to be moved; he who keeps thee will not slumber. Behold, he who keeps Israel shall neither slumber nor sleep. The Lord is thy keeper; the Lord is thy shade upon thy right hand. The sun shall not smite thee by day, nor the moon by night. The Lord shall preserve thee from all evil; he shall preserve thy soul. The Lord shall preserve thy going out and thy coming in from this time forth, and even for evermore." What a great promise.

"My Help"

Unto the hills, unto the skies, unto the hills, I will lift my eyes
To seek my God who does not sleep,
To seek my God, who always keeps me striving.

> *My help comes from the Father;*
> *My help comes from the Lord,*
> *My help comes from God, who suspends the stars above*
> *By His love, by His love.*

He will not slumber, He does not rest,
He's always there giving out His best,
He gives me peace; He gives me hope,
He gives me strength to help me cope when I don't feel like trying.

> *My help comes from the Father;*
> *My help comes from the Lord,*
> *My help comes from God, who suspends the stars above*
> *By His love, by His love.*

When I walk with God, there is no fear
Neither high nor low, far or near.
When I walk with God, He makes it clear—
My help is near, my help is near

> *My help comes from the Father;*
> *My help comes from the Lord,*

John M. Reichert

My help comes from God, who suspends the stars above
By His love, by His love.
Unto the hills, unto the skies,
unto the hills, I will lift my eyes.

OCTOBER '90

My friend, Steve, who I have mentioned before, and I were playing some music the other night, and we were discussing the fact that we have been playing and singing together for over fifty years now. What a tremendous blessing to have a friend like that. When we get together, Steve always requests that we sing "Just Like Peter."

"Just Like Peter"

It was late that night, and the Savior was on trial,
So, I moved into the courtyard to be warmed by the fire,
When a woman that I did not know accused me with her stare,
"You were with the Nazarene, I know, I saw you there."

> *I was not with Him, I was not with Him,*
> *The one of whom you speak, I have not seen.*
> *I do not know Him, I do not know the man,*
> *I tell you, I do not know the Nazarene.*

The crowd began to settle, and I thought that all was well
When another pointed toward me and this story, he did tell,
"You were with the Healer; you were one of His men."
"You were there when He made the blind to see and the lame to walk again."

I was not with Him, I was not with Him,
The one of whom you speak I have not seen.
I do not know Him, I do not know the man,
I tell you, I do not know the Nazarene.

Just like Peter, I've been afraid to face the crowd;
Their noise grows so loud when they press in on me.
Just like Peter, I've been afraid to take a stand;
Live my life the way God planned and be the witness I was meant to be.

Just like Peter, I've been confronted eye to eye,
And the one who gave His life for me, I've knowingly denied.
But the Lord, in His compassion, made me strong when I was weak;
He never turned His eyes from me when salvation I did seek.

Now I'm with Him, now I'm with Him,
The one of whom you speak, I've truly seen.
Yes, I know Him, yes, I know the Man,
I tell you; I truly know the Nazarene.

NOVEMBER '90

My mom, late in life, was in a Rehab Center recovering from a fall where she had banged her head, developing a subdural hematoma. I went for a visit one day, and as I was walking down the hall, I noticed an old gentleman sitting in his room listening closely to his radio. It was only later, after Mom had passed in 1998, that a man and his wife from the church where Mom had attended told me that sometimes when they visited, she would ask them to read her a scripture. This is the song God gave me in November 1990... "Old Folks."

"Old Folks"

She sits alone at the window, stares outside for a friend,
She wonders when this loneliness will end.
Maybe someone will come by today, maybe they'll stay for a while,
Maybe they'll read from the scriptures and make her smile.

> *Old folks are people too, they need loving just like me and you,*
> *They need someone just to let them know that they care.*
> *Old folks still believe in God, still believe the truths of faith and love,*
> *Still know how to make this world a better place to be—*
> *O Lord, we need to see as old folks see.*

He sits alone by the radio, catching the evening news,
When did we lose control of what God lets us use?
He remembers a time so long ago, he remembers before the war,
But lately, it seems no one needs Him anymore.

> *Old folks are people too, they need loving just like me and you,*
> *They need someone just to let them know that they care.*
> *Old folks still believe in God, still believe the truths of faith and love,*
> *Still know how to make this world a better place to be—*
> *O Lord, we need to see as old folks see.*

Old folks see with eyes that love and care,
And when it hurts, old folks lend their ear.
There's tireless times that old folks find to give and give and give,
And that's the wisdom in the way that old folks live.

> *Old folks are people too, they need loving just like me and you,*
> *They need someone just to let them know that they care.*
> *Old folks still believe in God, still believe the truths of faith and love,*
> *Still know how to make this world a better place to be—*
> *O Lord, we need to see as old folks see; O Lord, help us see as old folks see.*

DECEMBER '90

In December 1990, while attending a small church in South Bend, Indiana, God had me scribe down six songs that were used in their Christmas musical "The King." The next six are those songs.

"I Am the King"

Whose armies have slain thousands, whose power is unmatched,
Who reigns throughout the empire, and who controls the tax?
No one dare contest Me; no replacement do I need,
For as I raise my scepter, I issue the decree.

>*I am the King, I am the King,*
>*Great and Mighty is My throne; about Me, songs they sing,*
>*For I Am the King.*

No baby born shall take my throne; no child my rule shall have,
And by my power, I'll strike Him down and wipe Him from the land.
I will reign forever and sit upon the throne,
I am the King, I am the King, I am the King alone.

>*I am the King, I am the King,*
>*Great and Mighty is My throne; about Me, songs they sing,*
>*For I Am the King.*

I am the King, I am the King,
Great and Mighty is My throne; about Me, songs they sing,
For I Am the King.

"This Is My Son"

Such a lowly place, a King to grace,
A place where cattle feed,
A blessed boy to bring such joy,
The foretold David's seed.

> *This is my son, line of Jesse,*
> *Son of David, Son of God,*
> *Emmanuel, Mighty Savior, and this is my Son.*

This is the place, I shall see His face,
No gold or marble halls.
Such a lowly place, no palace gates,
Just a manger filled with straw.

> *Yes, this is my Son, line of Jesse,*
> *Son of David, Son of God,*
> *Emmanuel, Mighty Savior, and this is my Son.*

> *He will be a carpenter like His father,*
> *He will be one who builds with His hands,*
> *He will fill a church, He will fill a kingdom,*
> *And the church forever will it stand.*

This is my Son, line of Jesse,
Son of David, Son of God
Emmanuel, Mighty Savior, and this is my Son
And this is my Son.

"He Is the King"

A baby, such a fragile being, here before the King of eternity,
Savior of our people, King forevermore.
And this is, as the angel said, Jesus Christ the Lord.

> *He is the King, He is the King,*
> *Now that I've seen His face, my doubt's erased;*
> *I believe this thing—*
> *That He is the King.*

A ruler, where will His kingdom be,
Nazareth, near the sea of Galilee,
King of Kings, the Mighty, as the prophets have foretold—
This is, as the angel said, Jesus Christ the Lord.

> *He is the King, He is the King,*
> *Now that I've seen His face, my doubt's erased;*
> *I believe this thing—*
> *That He is the King*

> *He is the King, He is the King,*
> *Now that I've seen His face, my doubt's erased;*
> *I believe this thing—*
> *That He is the King.*

I love the Star Story of the Christmas season. I was blessed that God let me scribe this song, one of my favorites.

"Star of Bethlehem"

The journey has ended such a long, long way we've come,
At last, we're before Him; surely, He is the Chosen One.
A star by which to follow was set within the night,
Its brightness never dimming, it came to be our guide.

> *Star of Bethlehem has brought me where I am,*
> *Star of Bethlehem has brought me where I am—*
> *To my knees before the newborn King of Kings;*
> *Star of Bethlehem,*
> *Star of Bethlehem.*

Where did it come from? Observed throughout the sky
Bright Star of the Morning—it must be from God on high.
A star to place the Savior that we might know it's Him,
A star by God the Father, the Star of Bethlehem.

> *Star of Bethlehem has brought me where I am,*
> *Star of Bethlehem has brought me where I am—*
> *To my knees before the Mighty King of Kings.*

> *Star of Bethlehem has brought me where I am,*
> *Star of Bethlehem has brought me where I am—*
> *To my knees, to please the King of Kings;*
> *Star of Bethlehem,*
> *Star of Bethlehem.*

"Shepherds of Hebron"

We are shepherds of Hebron come to worship the King,
Come to offer our service and His praises to sing.

> *King of Kings, Lord of Lords,*
> *Prince of Peace, Father's Word.*

We are Shepherds of Hebron, come to worship the King.

We are sheep of the Shepherd, the Messiah we seek,
And the words of the angels, in secret, we keep.

> *King of Kings, Lord of Lords,*
> *Prince of Peace, Father's Word.*

We are sheep of the Shepherd, the Messiah we seek.

> *He is the Lilly of Valleys,*
> *He is the Prophet foretold,*
> *He is the Shepherd of children,*
> *He is the Lord.*

We are shepherds of Hebron come to worship the King,
Come to offer our service and His praises to sing.

> *King of Kings, Lord of Lords,*
> *Prince of Peace, Father's Word.*

We are Shepherds of Hebron, come to worship the King,
We are Shepherds of Hebron, come to worship the King.

John M. Reichert

"Glory to God"

The glory of God has filled the earth,
Glory to God, Glory to God.
The angels on high proclaim His birth,
Glory to God, Glory to God.

Born today to fulfill God's word,
Glory to God, Glory to God.
A Savior, which is Christ the Lord,
Glory to God, Glory to God.

Glory, Glory, Glory to God in the highest,
Let the heavens rejoice, Glory to God.
Glory, Glory, Glory to God in the Highest,
Fill the earth with His praise, Glory to God.

The glory of God has filled the earth,
Glory to God, Glory to God.
The angels on high proclaim His birth,
Glory to God, Glory to God.

Born today to fulfill God's word,
Glory to God, Glory to God.
A Savior, which is Christ the Lord,
Glory to God, Glory to God.

Glory, Glory, Glory to God in the Highest,
Let the heavens rejoice, Glory to God.
Glory, Glory, Glory to God in the Highest,
Fill the earth with His praise, Glory to God.

FEBRUARY '91

I must have been exhausted from December's scribing because there were none in January 1991. However, February brought two songs, "Coming Home," a song about Israel coming back to the promised land, and "He Gave His Life For Me," an obvious tune about Christ's death for me, a sinner.

"Coming Home"

They came from everywhere, around the world,
They came to see the Star as the flag unfurled,
They came across the sea to Palestine,
They came the land to free that God designed.

They came from suffering, they came from fear,
Some came from far away, and some were near.
They fought the Holy War of Jerusalem,
They joined together to keep the Holy Land.

> *Coming Home, Coming Home*
> *To a land that they may someday call their own.*
> *Coming Home, Coming Home—*
> *All the children of the Lord are coming home.*

Given to Abraham so many years ago,
The children wandered, with no place as a home.
Still, they came across the sea in 1948
To form a brotherhood, to form a state.

> Coming Home, Coming Home
> To a land that they may someday call their own.
> Coming Home, Coming Home—
> All the children of the Lord are coming home.
>
> Hear O Israel, the Lord our God is One;
> He has kept His promise by His one and only Son.
> Hear O Israel, the Lord our God is One;
> We will be His people, and He will be our God.

And in the final days, He'll gather up the world,
All the seed of Abraham, and all who have not heard.
They'll come to Palestine across the sea
To kneel before the judge on bended knees.

> Coming Home, Coming Home
> To a land that they may someday call their own.
> Coming Home, Coming Home—
> All the children of the Lord are coming home.
>
> All the children of the Lord are coming home.

"He Gave His Life For Me"

A lamb with dirty wool, before the shepherd stood,
The time of sacrifices began.
Though blemishes were seen, the Shepherd said, "He's clean,
For I can see the purity within."

   He gave His life for me, He gave His life for me,
   They nailed Him to a tree, and now my soul's been cleaned.
   He gave His life for me.

A prisoner in chains had caused so many pain;
His penalty required that he must die.
There was another plan, the Judge said, "Free this man,
For I will pay the price to save his life."

   He gave His life for me, He gave His life for me,
   They nailed Him to a tree, and now my soul's set free.
   He gave His life for me.

   What a wonderful thing to be purchased by a King
   And bow before His throne and give Him praise.
   What a wonderful day when you rise and hear Him say,
   "The cost has all been counted, here remain."

The captive and the lamb, they are a single man
Whose heart was bound by darkness and sin.
But the Father gave His Son, that bindings come undone,
And never more the darkness enter in.

   He gave His life for me, He gave His life for me,
   They nailed Him to a tree and now my soul's set free.
   He gave His life for me,
   He gave His life for me.

John M. Reichert

APRIL '91

In April 1991, God had me scribe down "The Bridge." This is a song about that gap between God and men. John 14:6 (KJV) says, "Jesus saith unto him (Thomas), I am the way, the truth, and the life: no man cometh unto the Father, but by me." Ever been to the Grand Canyon? The gulf between God and man is infinitely lager than that. Jesus is the only way to cross. Jesus is the bridge. Do not be undecided as the person in this song!

"The Bridge"

Here I am, on the edge, looking out across the chasm deep and wide,
And I wonder, from this ledge, how will I ever reach the other side?
I could jump, but I would fall, and death waits at the bottom for us all,
I looked left, I searched right, there was no way to cross within my sight.

> *To where God Most High, in His holiness, resides,*
> *Where Jesus sits alone at His right hand,*
> *Where children sing and the harps of angels ring,*
> *Where the lion is lying with the lamb.*

I asked a friend and engineer, is there any way to get to there from here?
He said, "No, it's far too wide, I don't think we'll ever reach the other side."
Then a man of faith came up to me; he said, "Son, there is a bridge you cannot see,
But there's a cost that must be paid before you walk the bridge and go your way."

> *To where God Most High, in His holiness, resides.*
> *Where Jesus sits alone at His right hand.*
> *Where children sing and the harps of angels ring.*
> *Where the lion is lying with the lamb.*

What is the fee, what must I do? The man of faith said, "Son, the toll's been paid for you.
It is God's Son, it is the Christ, who died that we might have a bridge to Life."
"And it's by faith, you must believe and step out on the bridge you cannot see;
The way is narrow, the path is straight, and it leads you to the pearly kingdom gates."

> *Where God Most High, in His holiness, resides,*
> *Where Jesus sits alone at His right hand,*
> *Where children sing and the harps of angels ring,*
> *Where the lion is lying with the lamb.*

> *Here I am, on the edge, looking out across the chasm deep and wide;*
> *I can't decide, I can't decide.*

John M. Reichert

The hundred-year-old hymn "Great Is Thy Faithfulness" is just awesome. Written by Thomas O. Chisholm in 1923, it expresses how God's love never ends. There is no turning with God.

Great Is Thy Faithfulness

Great is thy faithfulness, O God my Father,
there is no shadow of turning with thee.
Thou changes not, thy compassions, they fail not;
as thou hast been, thou forever wilt be.

> *Great is thy faithfulness! Great is thy faithfulness!*
> *Morning by morning new mercies I see;*
> *All I have needed thy hand hath provided.*
> *Great is thy faithfulness, Lord, unto me!*

Summer and winter and springtime and harvest,
sun, moon, and stars in their courses above
join with all nature in manifold witness
to thy great faithfulness, mercy, and love.

> *Great is thy faithfulness! Great is thy faithfulness!*
> *Morning by morning new mercies I see;*
> *All I have needed thy hand hath provided.*
> *Great is thy faithfulness, Lord, unto me!*

Pardon for sin and a peace that endureth,
thine own dear presence to cheer and to guide,
strength for today and bright hope for tomorrow,
blessings all mine, with ten thousand beside!

Great is thy faithfulness! Great is thy faithfulness!
Morning by morning new mercies I see;
All I have needed thy hand hath provided.
Great is thy faithfulness, Lord, unto me!

John M. Reichert

MAY '91

In May of 1991, God gave me "On and On" to scribe. It also expresses how God's love just keeps rolling on. No matter what is going on in your life, know that God is a God of love, He is in control, and His love never ends.

Lamentations 3:22–24 (NCV) says, "The Lord's love never ends; his mercies never stop. They are new every morning…"

"On and On"

You say you're down on your luck, don't know how to cope,
Don't know where your daily bread will come from, all out of hope.
Let me tell you this, my friend, God's love will never end;
He knows the trials that you are facing, He continues His Love—
O, on and on goes God's love.

> *God's love goes on and on.*
> *Like the waters of Old Man River, it keeps rolling along.*
> *Like a song that sticks in your mind,*
> *Got to be thinking 'bout it all the time—God's love goes on and on.*

I hear Zachary's got the flu, Erin's got the mumps,
There's three feet of water in the basement, the sump pump won't pump.

Let me say now, don't despair—out there's a God that cares.
He keeps raining down His love from above—
O, on and on goes God's love.

> *God's Love goes on and on.*
> *Like the waters of Old Man River, it keeps rolling along.*
> *Like a song that sticks in your mind,*
> *Got to be thinking 'bout it all the time—*
> *God's love goes on and on.*

Remember a man named Job and how he suffered so,
How it seemed that he'd been beaten.
He let his patience show, trusted in God's control;
God's love replaced the years that the locust had eaten.

> *God's love goes on and on.*
> *Like the waters of Old Man River, it keeps rolling along.*
> *Like a song that sticks in your mind,*
> *Got to be thinking 'bout it all the time—*
> *God's love goes on and on.*
>
> *God's love goes on and on and on and on and on and on.*

John M. Reichert

JUNE '91

*If one prevail against him, two shall withstand him;
and a threefold cord is not quickly broken.*

— Ecclesiastes 4:12 (KJV)

After a sermon on this passage and the truth that if two are bound together with the Lord, making three, God gave me this song to scribe.

"Bound Together"

*Two together can be unbreakable, bound together in the Lord.
When two in prayer and love are joined together, they are
Bound together in the Lord.*

> *Like a rope that will fray when tested alone,
> When entwined in a braid remains strong.*

*Two together can be unbreakable, bound together in the Lord.
When two in prayer and love are joined together, they are
Bound together in the Lord.*

> *Like a candle alone brightens not the heart,
> When matched with the light of love,
> Dispels the dark.*

Two together can be unbreakable, bound together in the Lord.
When two in prayer and love are joined together, they are
    Bound together in the Lord.

> *Like a note on the page whose meaning is lost,*
> *When combined, there's a way*
> *To make a beautiful song like*
>
> *You and I will last forever*
> *Bound together in the Lord.*
> *On and on, our love grows stronger*
> *Bound together in the Lord.*

Two together can be unbreakable, bound together in the Lord.
When two in prayer and love are joined together, they are
Bound together in the Lord.

John M. Reichert

JULY '91

First Chronicles 16:33 (KJV) says, "Then the trees of the wood sing out at the presence of the Lord, because he cometh to judge the earth."

I have hiked through many forests from the Smokey Mountains, Upper Lower Michigan, and Rocky Mountain National Park. If each tree is an individual voice, what a great chorus it will be when Christ comes to rule the earth. Go stand in the middle of a forest and listen to the trees!!

"Crown of Crowns"

There's a day coming soon that the world has not seen.
When the sky will open up and reveal the King of Kings
And the trumpet will sound and the Lord will appear;
He will wear the Crown of Crowns and reign for a thousand years.

> *I want to see the Crown of Crowns on the King of Kings,*
> *I want to see the Lord of Lords rule the world.*
> *I want to hear the mountains sound, listen to the forests sing,*
> *I want to see the Crown of Crowns on the King of Kings.*

Yes, the faithful will rise and stand before the Lord
To receive the crown of life as their reward.

But the glory that shines from the crown of the Lord
Will serve as a reminder of the suffering that He bore.

> *I want to see the Crown of Crowns on the King of Kings,*
> *I want to see the Lord of Lords rule the world.*
> *I want to hear the mountains sound, listen to the forests sing,*
> *I want to see the Crown of Crowns on the King of Kings.*

His crown of thorns has been replaced with a crown of gold
When He defeated death and ascended to His throne.
Yes, He's coming back with the kingdom through the air;
He'll be wearing the Crown of Crowns—there's no other that compares.

> *I want to see the Crown of Crowns on the King of Kings,*
> *I want to see the Lord of Lords rule the world.*
> *I want to hear the mountains sound, listen to the forests sing,*
> *I want to see the Crown of Crowns on the King of Kings.*

John M. Reichert

AUGUST '91

When my daughter Erin was little, her mother and I were walking through the mall one evening. I went into one store, and her mother went into a different store, both thinking the other person had our daughter. Neither of us did. Then panic set in. Fortunately, over the loudspeaker, we heard, "Will the parents of Erin Reichert please come to the information booth? We have your child." I raced to the booth. Asking how she got there, the attendant said a young man wearing a Notre Dame jacket found her alone and brought her to the booth. Erin was with her mother then, and I raced to find the angel wearing the ND jacket. They were nowhere to be found. Angels just disappear like that. This wasn't Erin's fault at all, but it did bring me to think that sometimes, as children of God, we get distracted by the world and let go of God's hand.

"Is It Too Late"

Have you seen Him, the one who left the footprints on the shore of Galilee?
I'd like to follow, but the water's erased them. Can you show the way to me?
You see, I'm dying; I've got leprosy.
I hear the Healer is the one who can set me free.

Is it too late to find the Savior?
Is it too late to ask a favor?
Of the one who fed the thousands from the mountainside,
Of the one who calmed the waters for a peaceful ride,
Of the one who caused the deaf to hear, who caused the blind to see—
Is it too late to work a miracle in me?

Have you seen Him, the one who bares the nail prints, in the middle of His hands?
I'd like to follow and be a disciple, but there are some things I just don't understand.
I saw Him crucified just the other day;
Now they say He's risen, and He's going away.

Is it too late to find the Savior?
Is it too late to ask a favor?
Of the one who fed the thousands from the mountainside,
Of the one who calmed the waters for a peaceful ride,
Of the one who caused the deaf to hear, who caused the blind to see—
Is it too late to work a miracle in me?

Have you seen Him, the one I call my Savior; seems I've lost my way again.
Like a child who gets distracted by the world, I must've let go of His hand.
So, I'm standing here, reaching out to find—
He's been waiting, standing there all the time.

Is it too late to find the Savior?
Is it too late to ask a favor?

John M. Reichert

Of the one who fed the thousands from the mountainside,
Of the one who calmed the waters for a peaceful ride,
Of the one who caused the deaf to hear, who caused the blind
  to see—
Is it too late to work a miracle in me?

It isn't too late to work Your miracles in me.

OCTOBER '91

O sing to the Lord a new song, sing unto the Lord all the earth.

— Psalm 96:1 (KJV)

I don't think that God gets upset if we plagiarize His word.

"Sing to the Lord"

Sing to the Lord a new song,
Sing to the Lord all the earth,
Sing of His infinite mercy
And His love that forever endures.

> *Let's raise the roof of the building*
> *and shatter the windows with sound,*
> *Spread the good news about Jesus,*
> *talk the Word all over town.*

Sing to the Lord a new song,
Sing to the Lord all the earth,
Sing of His infinite mercy
And His love that forever endures.

> *Echo your voice through the canyons,*
> *sing to the desert so dry,*

> Tell how God's Son came to save us,
> and on calvary's cross, He died.

Sing to the Lord a new song,
Sing to the Lord all the earth,
Sing of His infinite mercy
And His love that forever endures.

> Sing from the top of the mountain,
> sing from the valley so low,
> Sing how the grave's mouth was opened,
> and on the third day, He arose.

Sing to the Lord a new song,
Sing to the Lord all the earth,
Sing of His infinite mercy
And His love that forever endures.

> But the one who died and arose
> will one day return from above
> To gather secure in His kingdom
> all who remain in His love.

Sing to the Lord a new song,
Sing to the Lord all the earth,
Sing of His infinite mercy
And His love that forever endures.

I will sing, I will sing, I will sing to the Lord a new song;
I will sing, I will sing, I will sing to the Lord a new song.

NOVEMBER '91

In November of 1991, I spent a few days in the big city of Indianapolis for a sales job I was working. It was while in the city—with all the sirens and noise all around—when God gave me this song. November 1991 song "Only When."

"Only When"

Everybody seems pressed for decisions:
The answer's yes, the answer's no.
People always looking in the distance—
    Do I stay, or do I go?

The city streets are filled with confusion,
All around me, the noise swells.
People seem to be lost in illusion,
If somebody's leading, I cannot tell.

    Only when you come and listen,
    Only when your heart is still,
    Only when your voice is silent,
    Only then you can know God's will.

People running in the wrong direction;
Everybody tries to get ahead.
People living with the wrong intentions;
They don't love their brothers—it's themselves instead.

Only when you come and listen,
Only when your heart is still,
Only when your voice is silent,
Only then you can know God's will.

How can you find your way
In a world filled with darkness?
How will you know just where to go?

So many things we use to distract us,
So many reasons we lose the way.
A simple case of over enactment
With so little time left to hear God say.

Only when you come and listen,
Only when your heart is still,
Only when your voice is silent,
Only then you can know My will.

JANUARY '92

I love Bible stories in the Old Testament. Daniel in the lion's den, David and Goliath, Samson are just a few. Why not throw them all together in a song to start the new year off?

"One Desire"

Moses said to Pharoah, "Let God's people go."
Pharoah said to Moses, "Read my lips—NO, NO, NO."
Moses said that they must leave, that they may worship their
    Lord;
Pharoah said that might be true, "but it will not be by my word."

Nine object lessons later, Pharoah felt the same.
Hardened toward the children and the God that they proclaimed.
Then the angel of the Lord came down and took his only son;
Pharoah called to Moses and said, "Be gone, gone, gone."

From the Land of Goshen into the Sinai,
Moses led the people, led the people day and night.
The people cried from hunger; the people cried from thirst.
Moses said, "If you want to be fed, you've got to put Jehovah first."

> *He'll stand before you like a pillar of cloud,*
> *Guiding your footsteps, driving your enemies out.*
> *He'll come behind you like a pillar of fire;*
> *He's the one who keeps you—make Him your One Desire.*

John M. Reichert

Think about young Daniel, down in the lion's den;
He looked around with a frown and counted eight, nine, ten.
Daniel folded his hands together and offered up a prayer,
And in the morning, when the guards came around, they found
    Daniel standing there.

> God stood before him like a pillar of cloud,
> Filled the lion's bellies, shut the lion's mouth.
> He came behind him like a pillar of fire;
> Daniel knew who kept him, made Him his One Desire.

Shadrach, Meshach, Abednego, bow down they would not.
Nebuchadnezzar said, "Stoke the fire and make it Hot, Hot, Hot."
Four, it seemed, were walking in the fire, singing, giving praise
Nebuchadnezzar said, "Your God is God," when they stepped out
    of the blaze

> God stood before them like a pillar of cloud,
> Burnt the bindings off their hands from the fire, He brought
>   them out.
> He stood behind them like a pillar of fire;
> He's the One who kept them; they made Him their One
>   Desire.

So, no matter what befalls you, no matter what trouble comes,
Persevere—He's always near—keep your heart upon the One.
Like David against the giant and Samson with hair so long,
God will see you through every test and make you strong, strong,
    strong.

> He'll stand before you like a pillar of cloud,
> Guiding your footsteps, driving your enemies out.

He'll come behind you like a pillar of fire;
He's the one who keeps you—make Him your One Desire.

FEBRUARY '92

February is not usually the time to write an Easter song, but God laid this on my heart.

"All In All"

With one word, He spoke, and time began;
from darkness, the new world shone.
Then in His image, He created man
and called him unto His own.

> *Let us praise Him, praise Him,*
> *Praise God, the Father of all.*
> *Let us praise Him, praise Him*
> *By giving our all in all.*

God gave His Son to all mankind;
God gave His only Son
That man would choose from death to life
and bow and worship the One.

> *Let us praise Him, praise Him,*
> *Praise God, the Father of all.*
> *Let us praise Him, praise Him*
> *By giving our all in all.*

God gave to us a most perfect gift.
What have you done in return?
Have you given to Him all that comes from within?
O, what have you given to Him?

With one word, He spoke, and life began;
ARISE and come from the grave;
Death has lost its upper hand,
and all who believe will be saved.

> *Let us praise Him, praise Him,*
> *Praise God, the Father of all.*
> *Let us praise Him, praise Him*
> *By giving our all, giving our all,*
> *By giving our all in all.*

John M. Reichert

MARCH '92

The bases for this song came from an event that happened on a ski trip out west. When leaving the hotel, there was a man begging for a cup of coffee. It was obviously chilly out, and he wanted to get warmed up. One of the ladies in our party went over and gave the man a twenty-dollar bill. She told him not only to get a cup of coffee but to get a good hot meal. She certainly understood the concept that there are angels everywhere!!

"The Least of These"

I met him in a station, in Flagstaff, Arizona,
Waiting for the train to take me home.
It was plain to see he surely was a loner,
And all upon his back was all he owned.

He made his way around the room, asking for the small change,
But curses and abuse were all he found.
He caught my look through suffering eyes but carried still a soft smile;
He turned toward the door without a sound.

> *Somewhere in my memory, a Bible verse came back to me.*
> *This is what it had to say to me,*
> *"Unto the least of mine, feed the hungry, lead the blind,*

> *Open up your heart to those in need.*
> *Unto the least of mine, you'll never know just who you might find,*
> *You'll never know if it's the Son of Man you might see in the least of these."*

I followed into the cold night air, said, "Mister, there's something that I can spare."
Then I laid it softly in his hands,
I said, "You know it isn't much," but he held it with a gentle touch
Then pulled the sweater on, right over his.

> *And as he turned to walk away, I said, "I did not catch your name."*
> *He turned back with a smile, said, "Yes, you did."*

Rollin' on through Kansas, heading back to Indiana,
Twenty hours out, I fell asleep.
I dreamed a circle of angels, with singing and praise, were gathered,
But I could not tell to whom between their wings.

> *As the circle opened up, the tattered man stepped to the front;*
> *This is what He had to say to me,*
> *"Unto the least of Mine, you fed the hungry, led the blind,*
> *You opened up your heart to Me in need.*
> *Unto the least of Mine, you always knew just who you would find;*
> *You always knew that I, the Son of Man, you might see in the least of these."*

I met Him in a station in Flagstaff, Arizona, waiting for a train to take me home.

John M. Reichert

APRIL '92

I was thinking about a couple I knew in high school one day. He was a senior, and she was a sophomore. Their parents were against them seeing each other, and as so often happens, they would sneak off for secret meetings. They ended up having a baby and getting married. It worked out for many, many years.

"Safe In God's Hands"

They said we were too young to marry;
Kids out of school are not ready to start.
Ah, but we knew that God would be with us
Because we felt His love in our hearts.

They said, "What if you have a baby?
More mouths to feed will just tear you apart."
Ah, but we knew that God would teach us
Because we held His love in our hearts.

> *So many doubters before us;*
> *So few who gave us much chance.*
> *We kept holding on to each other*
> *While we placed our love safe in God's hands.*

They said that life won't be easy,
And sometimes, you'll just want to stop.

Ah, but we said we'd walk where God leads us
Because He held our love near His heart.

> *So many doubters before us;*
> *So few who gave us much chance.*
> *We kept holding on to each other*
> *While we placed our love safe in God's hands.*

And now, as we watch our youth fading
And the pages of life slowly pass,
Ah, we're still holding on to each other,
And our love's still safe in God's hands.

We're still holding each other,
And our love's still safe in God's hand.

John M. Reichert

JULY '92

Lights on a hill. A lot of talk about how America shines on a hill for all the world to see her greatness. Although recently, that light is fading—thanks to greedy, power-hungry politicians promoting a non-God-based agenda, the light barely twinkles. I was thinking about ordinary people who are lights on a hill every day.

"Lighthouse"

For sixty years, he's climbed the steps on the coast of Maine.
Three hundred sixty-three, he's counted; says he doesn't mind the rain.
He trims the wicks and lights the candles and shines the light out to sea,
So any wandering sailor—his way home, he might see.

For thirty years, he's climbed the steps and spoke the word out loud;
He's stood behind the wooden pulpit on the north side of town.
Though no one comes at alter call, still thirty years, he's still stayed,
Offers to those who wish to find the Truth, the Light, the Way.

> *You are a lighthouse to me, a light that I can see,*
> *A beam to set my course anew when sailing troubled seas.*
> *You give me strength to carry on and hope when I'm in need—*
> *You are a lighthouse to me.*

For thirteen years, she's raised the child, though most have been alone.
Her husband left a drunken man, but that was years ago.
Yet every Sunday finds them in church, learning what Jesus would do;
She says she's forgiven the "bottle-man" and hopes that you will too.

He says the news, "It isn't good," as he hangs up the phone.
The doctor says it's terminal, and soon he'd be gone.
So, he paints on his happy clown's face, heads to the children's home,
Said he had to make them laugh just one more time before he's heading on.

> *You are a lighthouse to me, a light that I can see,*
> *A beam to set my course anew when sailing troubled seas.*
> *You give me strength to carry on and hope when I'm in need—*
> *You are a lighthouse to me.*

For thirty years, He walked the earth and did His Father's will.
Though many saw Him crucified, I know He's living still.
He suffered much to pay the cost that God's grace might be free—
You are a lighthouse to me.

> *You are a lighthouse to me, a light that I can see,*
> *A beam to set my course anew when sailing troubled seas.*
> *You give me strength to carry on and hope when I'm in need—*
> *You are a lighthouse, You are a lighthouse, You are THE Lighthouse to me.*

John M. Reichert

Do you think Jesus looks at His nail-pierced hands, sees the scars, and smiles? Knowing that the price has been paid and that Satan and death have been defeated... I think He does.

"When You See the Scars"

When You see the scars, do You think about the pain?
From the suffering that You bore,
Do You hear the crowds of people call Your name,
Crying, "Crucify the Lord!"

When You see the scars, do You think about the time
When You drank a bitter cup?
And did You know that in giving up Your life
That You'd be lifted up?

> *O Lord, how matchless is Your name,*
> *Greater than all that ever was.*
> *Lord, when You see the marks upon your skin,*
> *Lord, see the scars as love.*

When You see the scars, do You think about the cross?
Do You think of all You gave?
When You see the scars, do You think about the cost?
The price You chose to pay?

> *O Lord, how matchless is Your name,*
> *Greater than all that ever was.*
> *Lord, when You see the marks upon your skin,*
> *Lord, see the scars as love.*

O Lord, how matchless is Your name,
Greater than all that ever was.
Lord, when You see the marks upon your skin,
Lord, see the scars as love.

John M. Reichert

AUGUST '92

The scars got me thinking about the time prior to His crucifixion, the time Christ spent in the Garden of Gethsemane. The agony must have been unbearable. In fact, the Bible tells us Jesus sweat drops of blood. I can't even imagine the anxiety of what He was about to face.

"Gethsemane"

To this garden, on a hilltop,
Among the flowers of Gethsemane,
Though my faithful fall behind Me,
I have come to plead with Thee.

> *Is there any other way that I can bring Your will about?*
> *Is there any other way that I might live?*
> *As I agonize the meaning,*
> *Sweat like blood upon My brow,*
> *Your will will be when I leave Gethsemane.*

In this garden, I am praying
For those who follow Me.
Fill their spirit with Your glory,
Though the world hates them as Me.

> *Is there any other way that I can bring Your will about?*
> *Is there any other way that I might live?*

> *As I agonize the meaning,*
> *Sweat like blood upon My brow,*
> *Your will will be when I leave Gethsemane.*

From this garden, they will take Me,
They'll spit and beat upon My face.
They will stripe Me, they will mock Me,
And I wish no one to take My place.

> *Because there isn't any other way that I can bring Your will about.*
> *Father, I resign Myself to die that they might live.*
> *Still, as I agonize this meaning,*
> *Sweat like blood upon My brow,*

As in Heaven, Your will will be.
As in Heaven, Your will will be, in Gethsemane.

John M. Reichert

SEPTEMBER '92

From the garden, the Roman soldiers took Jesus to trial.

"The Trial"

Who is this man who stands before me? What are the charges you bring?
Is He the one who claims to be Lord, the one who claims to be King?
Is it because He comes from Nazareth that you wish His death through me?
What would you say of all of His works had He been a Pharisee?

Is He the one who healed the sick and made the blind to see?
Is He the one who raised the dead, who walked on Galilee?
Is He the one who fed the thousands with a basket of fish and bread?
This man does no wrong; His works are all good, so why do you wish Him dead?

> *Outside, they cry, "Give us Barabbas!"*
> *Others cry, "Set this man free!"*
> *Outside, they cry, "Crucify Jesus!*
> *And shed His blood on the tree."*

Is it because He cleared the temple of the priest who bought and sold?
Is it because He calls Himself Son, the Son of the Ancient of Old?
Is it because so many follow, believe, and the numbers grow strong?
How can I rule in a trial such as this? The accused has done no wrong.

> *Outside, they cry, "Give us Barabbas!"*
> *Others cry, "Set this man free!"*
> *Outside, they cry, "Crucify Jesus!*
> *And shed His blood on the tree."*

What shall I do with this man called Jesus? Your envy grows into hate.
The King of the Jews offers no defense and answers, "As you say."
He humbles Himself before His Father; if not bound, He would fall to His knees.
End of the trial, I wash my hands of His blood, "Do with Him as you please."

> *Outside, they cry, "Give us Barabbas!"*
> *Spurred on by the Pharisees.*
> *Outside, they cry, "Crucify Jesus!"*
> *And fewer cried, "Set this man free!"*

> *Outside, they cried, "Give us Barabbas!*
> *Shed Jesus' blood on the tree."*
> *Outside, they cried, "Crucify Jesus,"*
> *so they set a murderer free.*

John M. Reichert

Who was this man who stood before me? Could He have truly been Son of God?
And how have I changed the course of time by handing Him to this mob?
What if He rises on the third day as the Jewish scribes wrote of old?
Then I've been a pawn, and this trial's been a tool of a story that's yet to be told;
Yes, I've been a pawn, and this trial's been a tool of a story that's yet to be told.

While Jesus was on trial, Peter, the Rock, was in the courtyard denying Jesus.

"Denied"

What would you do if it came right down to it? What would you say?
If someone pointed their finger at you, what would you say?
You've been seen talking to Jesus; you've been seen listening to Him;
What would you do if they singled you out and said, "You are one of His."

O faithful follower, what would you do, O what would you say
If an angry mob rose up against you, O what would you say?
You've been seen with the people of the teacher, you were there when He did those miracles;
What would you do if they singled you out and said, "You know those parables."

Would you stand firm? Would Jesus be denied?
Would you say I never knew him? Would you tell a lie?
Would it happen once, would it happen twice, would it happen maybe three times?
Before the coming of the morning light, would Jesus be denied?

Would you be just like Peter when forced to take a stand?
Would you become of a different nature and deny this man?
Peter didn't have the Holy Ghost to turn to; you, my friend, have a power deep inside;
What would you do if they singled you out? Oh, you better make up your mind.

Peter didn't stand firm; Jesus was denied.
Peter said I never knew him; Peter told a lie
You know it happened once, you know it happened twice,
You know it happened three times;
Before the coming of the morning light, Jesus was denied.

What will you say when it comes right down to it, O what will you say
When someone points their finger at you, O what will you say?
You've been seen praying to Jesus; you've been seen listening for replies;
What will you say when they single you out? Are you preparing to lie?

You must stand firm; Jesus don't deny.
You must say you truly know Him, don't tell a lie.
Don't let it happen three times, don't let it happen twice,

John M. Reichert

Don't even let it happen one time;
Before the coming of the morning light, don't let Him be denied.

Jesus spent a last supper with His disciples, where He broke bread and drank a cup of wine and explained to them what it all meant. The bread was His body that had to be broken, and the cup was His blood that had to be poured out for the forgiveness of sin. Jesus died for you, and He died for me. Let us remember His sacrifice.

"Take This Cup"

This feast of the Passover, as we celebrate,
Will be saddened by what I must say; it cannot wait.
I carry the knowledge of My death to come,
I know that I'm to be the sacrificed one.

> *Take this cup, poured out for many,*
> *Poured out for the forgiveness of sins.*
> *Take this cup, drink it in My memory,*
> *Partake of life eternally, with Me.*

I will be broken as the bread tonight;
My body, like the bread, will put up no fight.
Broken for you and all who believe,
Forgiveness for transgressions given through Me.

> *Take this cup, poured out for many,*
> *Poured out for the forgiveness of sins.*

> *Take this cup, drink it in My memory,*
> *Partake of life eternally, with Me.*

My life will be poured out like the wine from the cup,
The life from My body as they spill out My blood.
Poured out for you and all who believe,
In the life that My Father is giving through Me.

> *Take this cup, poured out for many,*
> *Poured out for the forgiveness of sins.*
> *Take this cup, drink it in My memory,*
> *Partake of life eternally.*

> *When we drink this cup again together,*
> *We will drink it in the kingdom,*
> *With our Father, with our Holy Father.*

> *Take this cup, poured out for many,*
> *Poured out for the forgiveness of sins.*
> *Take this cup, drink it in My memory,*
> *Partake of life eternally, with Me.*

John M. Reichert

DECEMBER '92

After Jesus had risen from the grave and before He ascended to heaven to be with His Father, He appeared to His disciples and gave them instructions. Go into all the world and preach the Gospel. I am sending you.

"Sending You"

So many people in a dying world,
so many people who have not heard the Word,
And if you love Me like you say you do,
go and feed My sheep; I am sending you.

So many deaf ears that cannot hear,
so many hearts bound up with fear,
So little time left, the wedding is near;
since you love Me, I am sending you

> *Sending You, I'm sending you,*
> *I'm sending you into all the lands.*
> *Sending You, I'm sending you,*
> *Sending you to feed My lambs.*

So many eyes that have not seen,
so many soiled garments to be cleaned;
The groom is ready, the feast is due;
with invitations, I am sending you.

Sending You, I'm sending you,
I'm sending you into all the lands.
Sending You, I'm sending you,
Sending you to feed My lambs.

Tell the world the kingdom is coming,
A wedding feast is about to be shared.
Tell the world a new day is dawning—
It's because of the Father who cares.

So many people in a dying world,
so many people who have not heard the Word,
And if you love Me like you say you do,
go and feed My sheep; I am sending you.

Sending You, I'm sending you,
I'm sending you as with nail-pierced hands.
Sending You, I'm sending you,
Sending you into all the lands.

Sending You, I'm sending you,
I'm sending you into all the lands.
Sending You, I'm sending you,
Sending you to feed My lambs.

It wouldn't be Christmas time without a Christmas song.

John M. Reichert

"A Child From Bethlehem"

He walked away from the trash barrel fire at the corner Clark and Main,
Made his way toward the mission hope, the sky began to rain.
He passed the local barber shop by the First United Church,
Though the doors were closed, he was sure he heard a choir rehearse.

Underneath the big, stained window stood a scene from Bethlehem,
A father, mother, wise men three, two shepherds, and a lamb.
As he looked into the manger straw, the baby wasn't there;
He mumbled low his words of pain, "Even Jesus doesn't care."

From the shadows stepped a little girl, baby Jesus in her arms.
She was dressed in winter's best, her scarf and mittens warm.
She told the man her daddy died just last Christmas eve,
So, she begged her mom to let her come and hold the baby, please.

> *She said, "A silent night, a holy night, a child from Bethlehem*
> *Was born so tiny and so small, yet grew to be a man*
> *To take away our suffering," that's what her daddy had said,*
> *"If you hold on to Him tight, He'll give you hope and peace and rest."*

The old man said, "I've been sad too since I lost my family.
A wife, a little girl like you—guess I've lost everything."
She reached and held his dirty hand and squeezed his fingers tight,
Said here, "Please hold the baby, sir; He'll make you feel all right."

She asked him if he'd sing with her her favorite Christmas song,
So, a-cappella, hand in hand, the old man sang along.
Out of tune and gravely, their voices seemed to clash
With those who sang inside the church, behind the painted glass.

> *Silent night, holy night, all is calm, all is bright*
> *Round yon virgin, mother and child, holy infant so tender and mild*
> *Sleep in heavenly peace, sleep in heavenly peace.*[2]

The man and girl went separate ways, the girl toward her home,
The man toward the Mission Hope; the sky began to snow.
He could not forget the manger scene and all that was given to him—
A chance for hope and rest and peace by a child from Bethlehem

> *A silent night, a holy night, a child from Bethlehem*
> *Was born so tiny and so small, yet grew to be a man*
> *To take away our suffering, that's what the little girl had said,*
> *"If you hold on to him tight, He'll give you hope and peace and rest."*
>
> *Silent night, Holy night, Son of God, love's pure light.*
> *Radiant beams from thy Holy face, with the dawn of redeeming grace,*
> *Jesus, Lord at thy birth, Jesus, Lord at thy birth.*

---

[2] "Silent Night" composed by Franz Gruber, lyrics by Joseph Mohr.

APRIL '93

If you are not ALWAYS on guard, Satan will try to trick you into sinning. Satan is the great Deceiver. If that happens, and we all do, repent immediately and ask God to forgive you, and with the grace of God, next time, it won't be so easy for Satan to trip you up.

"Next Time"

Just when I think the battle's over,
Just when I think that I will win,
Satan reaches up and trips me over,
That's the time that I most likely sin, so I pray:

> *"Lord, next time, help me not to give in,*
> *Help my feet to flee from sin,*
> *Help me be more watchful,*
> *Help me to be stronger,*
> *Help me be more faithful,*
>   *Next Time."*

Just when I think the storm is clearing,
Just when the sun comes shining through,
Thunder on horizons starts appearing,
That's the time I lift my voice to You, and I pray:

"Lord, next time, help me not to give in,
Help my feet to flee from sin,
Help me be more watchful,
Help me to be stronger,
Help me be more faithful,
   Next Time."

"Help me be more watchful,
Help me to be strong,
Help me be more faithful all day long,
Help me be more watchful,
Help me to be stronger,
Help me be more faithful,
   Next Time."

John M. Reichert

MAY '93

In May 1993, God gave me an instrumental called "When I'm Alone." There are no lyrics, so it cannot be printed here.

Also, in May 1993, God gave me "The Power of God." I have been blessed to stand on mountain tops and at the bottom of the Grand Canyon, the edge of the Pacific and Atlantic Oceans, and there is always that overwhelming sense of power that I feel from my Creator.

"The Power of God"

I've stood on the top of the mountain,
I've watched the sun come up,
I've seen the northern lights dancing with the stars,
I've seen the mighty Power of my God of love;
I've seen the mighty Power of my God.

I've stood on the edge of the ocean,
Ridden on the crest of the swell.
I've seen Him take a raging sea and turn it into glass.
His peace has touched my soul as well, as well;
His peace has touched my soul as well.

> *I will sing, I will sing,*
> *I will sing of the Power of my God.*
> *I will sing, I will sing,*
> *I will sing of the Power of my God.*

I stood at the bottom of the canyon
Carved by the finger of His hand.
Every word that man has ever spoken of this place
Is attributed to my God so Grand, so Grand.
His power makes my God so Grand.

> *I will sing, I will sing,*
> *I will sing of the Power of my God.*
> *I will sing, I will sing,*
> *I will sing of the Power of my God.*

I've stood in the darkness of sin and shame,
I was lost in the blackness of the night.
The Power of my God that raised His Son up from the dead
Drove the darkness back and set me in the light of lights.
Drove the darkness back and set me in the light.

> *I will sing, I will sing,*
> *I will sing of the Power of my God.*
> *I will sing, I will sing,*
> *I will sing of the Power of my God.*

John M. Reichert

JUNE '93

In June 1993, there was another instrumental titled "More Than a Friend." As I was sitting on the back porch one evening, I was watching a moth fluttering around the light bulb. That little moth has the whole universe to go fly around in, but he was drawn to the light.

"Drawn to the Light"

Living without Jesus is like traveling through a tunnel,
Looking for the light at the end of your way,
Stumbling in the darkness, in and out of trouble,
You offer prayers at nighttime, look for answers in the day.

But up ahead in the distance, you see a brightness that you can't explain,
You set your gaze with a fixedness, press on through the darkness,
Press on through the pain, you are...

> *Drawn to the light, like a moth in the nighttime.*
> *Drawn to the brightness and the warmth.*
> *Drawn to the light, it will open your eyesight*
> *And take off the blindness that you wore.*

Living without Jesus is like sailing without a wheel:
No way to guide the rudder, the ship begins to reel.

Drifting, no direction, no way for you to steer,
You hear the breakers sounding; the rocks of death are near.

Up ahead in the distance, near the shore, you see a shining light,
You finally come to your senses; you set out in a life raft,
Leave that sinking ship behind; you are…

> *Drawn to the light, drawn to the brightness,*
> *Drawn to the safety of the shore,*
> *Drawn to the light, drawn to the rightness,*
> *Jesus gives you so much more.*

The world is filled with things you don't understand,
But there's a light that shows the way.
He's standing, reaching with an open hand.
Reach for Jesus, reach for Jesus, reach for Jesus today, and let yourself be…

> *Drawn to the light, drawn to the brightness,*
> *Drawn to the salvation of the Lord,*
> *Drawn to the light, drawn to the rightness,*
> *Jesus gives you so much more.*
> *Drawn to the light.*

John M. Reichert

JULY '93

I love to canoe. I love floating down a river, watching all the wildlife. It's peaceful. I love hiking in the mountains and through the desert. God's wonderful creation is awe-inspiring. It gives me joy, peace, and hope. First Peter 3:15 (KJV): "…be always ready to give an answer to every man that asketh you a reason of the hope that is in you…"

"Don't Go In the River"

Don't go in the river if you don't know how to swim ;
Don't crawl out of the safety of the life raft that you're in;
Don't climb up on a slippery rock if you know that you'll fall in;
Don't go in the river if you don't know how to swim.

> *Be prepared to explain all the joy that you have,*
> *Tell the world the reason that you're glad.*
> *Be prepared to account for the joy you have inside,*
> *Tell the world that Jesus in your heart resides.*

Don't start across the desert in the heat of the day;
If you don't know where the water holes, lie alone the way.
Don't leave your canteen in the car and think you'll be okay;
Don't start across the desert in the heat of the day.

> *Be prepared to explain all the peace that you have,*
> *Tell the world how that peace makes you glad.*

> *Be prepared to account for the peace you have inside,*
> *Tell the world that Jesus in your heart resides.*

Don't climb in the mountains if you don't know how to use the ropes,
If you don't know about crampons and traversing icy slopes.
You don't climb without a partner to belay you on a rope;
Don't climb in the mountains if you don't know how to use the ropes.

> *Be prepared to explain all the hope that you have,*
> *Tell the world how that hope makes you glad.*
> *Be prepared to account for the hope you have inside,*
> *Tell the world that Jesus in your heart resides.*

> *He is there, and you are happy;*
> *He is there, and He makes you smile.*
> *He is there, and He give you hope for the coming kingdom;*
> *He is there all the while.*

Don't go in the river if you don't know how to swim;
Don't crawl out of the safety of the life raft that you're in;
Don't climb up on a slippery rock if you know that you'll fall in;
Don't go in the river if you don't know how to swim.

John M. Reichert

SEPTEMBER '93

All my life, I wanted to be an astronaut. Then when I was eight, I broke the tip of my right elbow. No one had ever been to space with a broken bone, so I dropped out of the astronaut program! Later in life, I learned that some of the astronauts who had gone up with the space shuttle had broken bones as kids. I would go today if they would take me! Beam me up, Scotty!!! When I was a sophomore in high school, my dad and I were walking uptown. We were in front of the pharmacy, and he asked me what I was going to do with the rest of my life. He said, "Don't work in the same factory for forty years like me. Why don't you go to pharmacy school and be a pharmacist like Warren (our local pharmacist)?" I said, "Okay," and I was on the path. We had just passed the Mortuary when Dad asked me!! I could have been anything, but God wanted me to be a pharmacist and a minstrel.

"Lowly Soul"

I could have been a farmer boy with a tractor for a toy,
Planting seeds and making hay.
I could've been a surgeon skilled, lawyer writing wills,
And if I was, that's okay.
I could've been an engineer, building bridges near.
I could've been an astronaut;
Then I'd have been flying high, way up above the sky—
Guess what? I'm not.

> *I'm just a Lowly Soul, Lowly Soul,*
> *Sitting here playing the strings.*
> *I'm just a Lowly Soul, Lowly Soul,*
> *Doing my best for the King.*

I could've been an architect, building houses with a deck,
Watching them go up to the sky.
I could've been a Mister Mom, cleaning house all day long,
Chasing kids, and building their lives.
I could've been a soldier blue, fighting wars for you.
I could've been a preacher man;
Then I'd have been standing here, lifting up my prayers
with a Bible in my hand.

> *I'm just a Lowly Soul, Lowly Soul,*
> *Sitting here playing the strings.*
> *I'm just a Lowly Soul, Lowly Soul,*
> *Doing my best for the King.*

> *God said to choose the path that you will walk today,*
> *And He'll guide your footsteps all along the way.*

I chose to be a pharmacist, playing doctor with a twist,
Counting pills, making ointments, too.
I also chose the minstrel's role, singing songs from my soul—
That's why I'm here today with you.

> *I'm just a Lowly Soul, Lowly Soul,*
> *Sitting here playing the strings.*
> *I'm just a Lowly Soul, Lowly Soul,*
> *Doing my best for the King.*

John M. Reichert

NOVEMBER '93

This next song, from November 1993, comes directly from Psalm 139:7–13 (KJV). It's a good read and tells us that there is no place to hide from God.

"There Is No Place"

Where can I go to hide from Your spirit?
Where can I go to flee from You?
Surely the darkness, I thought it, would hide me,
Surely the night can hide me from You.

> *If I go into the heavens, You are there;*
> *If I go down to the depths, you are there.*
> *If I rise upon the wind and fly across the sea,*
> *Your hand will guide me; your eye will see.*

Where can I go to hide from Your spirit?
Where can I go to flee from You?
Surely the darkness, I thought it, would hide me,
Surely the night can hide me from You.

> *If I go into the mountains, You are there;*
> *If I hide deep in the caves, You are there.*
> *If I start across the wilderness, walk upon the sands,*
> *Your eye will see, you'll guide with Your hands.*

There's no place that I can go
That Your spirit cannot know.
There's no place that I can hide from You.

If I go into the city, You are there;
If I go into the country, You are there.
If I build the highest building, reach up to the sky,
Your hand will touch me, You'll see with Your eye.

There is no place to hide from Your spirit,
There is no place to flee from You.
There is no place, there is no place.

Psalm 23 talks about God guiding us like a Shepherd, with His staff, beside still waters and into green pastures. I've quoted this psalm in my heart many times when I needed to feel closer to my Great Shepherd. I have always found comfort and guidance!

"O Great Shepherd"

O Great Shepherd, I need green pastures,
I need Your loving rod and staff.
I need Your promise to love and guide me
As I travel from the past.

O Great Shepherd, I need still waters,
The drink you give each time I call.
I need the promise that You'll sustain me,
Pick me up each time that I fall.

> *I need the comfort of Your presence*
> *When on You, I need to lean.*
> *I need the strength I feel surround me*
> *When I know You take the lead.*

O Great Shepherd, I need Your wisdom
As I face the problems of the day.
I need your quiet, understanding
To complete this journey all the way.

> *I need the comfort of Your presence*
> *When on You, I need to lean.*
> *I need the strength I feel surround me*
> *When I know you take the lead.*

O Great Shepherd, touch and heal me,
Injured lamb within Your pen.
Tender care and love provide me,
Touch my heart and make me whole again;
Touch my heart and make me whole again.

JANUARY '94

The story of the ten lepers has always been one of my favorites. I just don't understand how nine of the lepers, after being completely healed physically, did not even give thanks to Jesus for the wonderful thing He did. Only the one who was made whole spiritually returned with praise. I pray that I am always the tenth leper.

"Ten Lepers"

Ten lepers sought out Jesus,
Faith and hope in His healing power.
Some were Jews, and some were strangers;
Sought Him out for hours and hours.

Found Him near Jerusalem
Going to a village small.
Healed the young and the old of age,
Touched and healed them one and all.

> *All ten lepers, washed and cleansed,*
> *Spots removed made whole again.*
> *Nine of ten went their own way,*
> *One came back to praise His name.*
> *Only one came back to praise His name.*

John M. Reichert

Ten Lepers sought out Jesus,
Found Him near Jerusalem.
Nine of ten went their own way,
One came back to praise His name.

> *All ten lepers, washed and cleansed,*
> *Spots removed made whole again.*
> *Nine of ten went their own way,*
> *One came back to praise His name.*
> *Only one came back to praise, His name.*

Ten lepers sought out Jesus,
Faith and hope in His healing power.
Some were Jews, and some were strangers;
Sought Him out for hours and hours,
Sought Him out for hours and hours.
Only one came back to praise His name.

FEBRUARY '94

Psalm 40:3 (KJV) says, "And He hath put a new song in my mouth, even praise unto our God; many shall see it, and fear, and shall trust in the LORD."

"New Song"

There's a new song, down in my heart, today, today,
I thought you might hear it right from the start.
In the way I sing, in the way I play,
O, O, New Song. O, O, New Song.

There are new words I need to sing, today, today,
About a risen, living King.
Who is coming back someday,
O, O, New Song. O, O, New Song.

> *I know He's coming back, He promised in His word*
> *There'll be joy and shouting like the world has never heard.*
> *Let us lift our voices up and strike up the chords*
> *Of the New Song.*

There's a new hope down deep inside,
Down in my soul, down in my soul.
Burns so hot, I just can't hide it,
So, I have to let the music roll.
O, O, New Song. O, O, New Song.

John M. Reichert

I know He's coming back, He promised in His word
There'll be joy and shouting like the world has never heard.
Let us lift our voices up and strike up the chords
Of the New Song.

There's a new song, down in my heart, today, today,
I thought you might hear it right from the start.
In the way I sing, in the way I play
O, O, New Song. O, O, New Song.

APRIL '94

God gave me from Psalm 96:11 (KJV): "Let the Heavens rejoice, and let the earth be glad; let the sea roar, and the fulness thereof."

"Rejoice"

Rejoice, Rejoice, Rejoice, Rejoice.

Like the wind and the sky, like the earth and the sea,
Rejoice as they kneel at the feet of the King,
Like the angels on high as they open their wings.

Rejoice, Rejoice, Rejoice, Rejoice.

Like the mountains, who bow down their heads to give praise,
Like the moon and the sun, who worship in days,
Like the flower that opens its petals in praise,

Rejoice, Rejoice, Rejoice, Rejoice.

> *Rejoice, rejoice all the earth and be glad,*
> *Rejoice and give praise with all that you have.*

Rejoice, unto the Lord; Rejoice, unto the Lord.
Rejoice, unto the Lord; Rejoice, unto the Lord.

Like the eagle that soars to the edge of the sky,
Like the song of the whale in the ocean it dives,

Like the voice of the newborn who opens and cries,

Rejoice, unto the Lord; Rejoice, unto the Lord.
Rejoice, unto the Lord; Rejoice, unto the Lord.

MAY '94

My first blues song came in May 1994. A tune called "Walkin." I didn't know how much fun it was going to be until we played it. One of Crooked Nail's members was a bass and rhythm guitar player who eventually started paying some blues leads! He loved this tune.

"Walkin'"

I've been walkin' with my Jesus day by day,
I've been walkin' with my Jesus day by day.
He whispers softly to me,
"You know I like it that way."

I've been walkin' with my Jesus side by side,
Yes, I've been walkin' with my Jesus side by side.
He says now, "Don't you worry,
All your needs I will provide."

When I get tired of walkin', my Jesus carries me awhile.
When I get tired of walkin', my Jesus carries me awhile

And though His arms be aching.
On His face, there is a smile.
Blues lead!!!

Well, He's building me a mansion in that kingdom in the sky,
He's building me a mansion in that kingdom in the sky.
And when He brings that kingdom back to earth,
Won't be no need for me to cry.

'Cause I'll be walkin' in that kingdom with my Lord,
Yes, I'll be walkin' in that kingdom with my Lord.
When He brings that kingdom back to earth,
Sin and death will be no more.

Yes, when He brings that kingdom back to earth,
There won't be any blues… anymore.

JUNE '94

I can't help being in awe of God when I'm in nature. Many would have you believe that most things in nature "just happened" to help a species survive or evolve to "the next level." I believe God has a purpose and a plan for every one of His creations. Psalm 145:10, Voice translation, says, "All creation will stand in awe of You, O Eternal One. Thanks will pour from the mouths of every one of Your creatures. Your holy people will bless You."

"Whenever I Think of You"

Whenever I think of You and all that You can be,
I know that my thoughts are true; You're everything to me.
Even in the darkest night, You are a shining star.
Whenever I think of You, I know just where You are.

Whenever I think of You and all that I believe,
I know that my faith is proved; Your grace envelopes me.
All of my simplest prayers You've provided for;
Whenever I think of You, I think of You as Lord.

> *All my worries disappear*
> *Whenever You reach and draw me near.*
> *All of my simplest needs You've provided for;*
> *Whenever I think of You, I think of You as Lord.*

John M. Reichert

Whenever I think of You and all that You have done,
All the love that You give to me, You gave Your only Son,
Whose silent love in death He gave and never once complained—
Whenever I think of You, I think Holy is Your Name.

Whenever I think of You, I think Holy is Your Name.

I was raised in the church. My parents were very strict about attending every Sunday morning and evening, Wednesday night, Bible study, and any other event where the church doors were open. There was no rock'n'roll music, dancing, smoking, or drinking. So, when I got to college, I wandered. It was Divine Providence for me that my parents believed the truth of Proverbs 22:6 (KJV): "Train up a child in the way he should go and when he is old, he will not depart from it." Thanks, Mon and Dad!

"Wandering Years"

Forty years wandering in the desert, not really knowing which
    way was home,
Hot sun, beating down on their heads, forced to roam and roam,
Then a fire, high upon the mountain, spoke and said, "I Am the
    One.
You have always been a people chosen, chosen to serve my Son."

> *After the wandering years,*
> *After the wandering years,*
> *After the wandering,*
> *After the wandering years.*

How bright shines the light in your eyes on the Damascus Road!
Can you see the path you left behind? Can you see the road you wandered on?
Can you say that you changed your point of view now that you've seen the light?
Can you tell me just what you're gonna do, are you gonna do, gonna do what's right?

> *After the wandering years,*
> *After the wandering years,*
> *After the wandering,*
> *After the wandering years.*

> *After the wandering years, where will you turn?*
> *Where will you go?*
> *After the wandering years, who will you serve?*
> *Who will you know?*
> *After the wandering years.*

All your life, you've been out upon the river, fighting that downstream flow,
Seems like you've always been caught up in the current, never able to reach the shore.
You've decided to finally stop your drifting; it's time to reach for the solid ground.
The river's fast, but the water is shallow. To make your stand, just put your feet on the ground.

> *Stop all the wandering years,*
> *Stop all the wandering years,*
> *Stop all the wandering, stop all the wandering years.*

John M. Reichert

I played in a contemporary Christian band called Crooked Nail. In 2002, we recorded a CD. The title of the CD was *Show Me the Way*. I scribed this song from God after my daughter Erin decided to give her life to follow Christ. That will make your heart sing!!

"Show Me the Way"

The road up ahead will be rough,
Filled with rocks and filled with ruts.
I don't always know which way I'm going.

Can't seem to find my way back home,
All my life it seems I've roamed and roamed,
But, O, Lord, You can show me.

> *Show me the way,*
> *Show me the way,*
> *Lord, You are the One who can guide me.*
> *You are the One who provides me*
> *And shows me the way.*

Sometimes the road is long and winding,
The sun is hot; the light is blinding;
All of my steps, they feel uncertain.

Danger lurks at each side of me,
The Devil nips my heels and tempts me,
Lord, only You can see around the next curve.

Show me the way,
Show me the way,
Lord, You are the One who can guide me.
You are the One who provides me
And shows me the way.

Show me the way,
Show me the way,
Lord, You are the One who can guide me.
You are the One who provides me
And shows me the way.

JULY '94

In July 1994, I was blessed once again to go backpacking into the mountains of Colorado. My true North, Rocky Mountain National Park. If you ever get the chance to stand on Long's Peak, 14,259 ft, do it. I've been up there three times, and each time, it was amazing. Like life, it is not easy to get there, but the struggle is so worth it.

"Off to the Mountains"

Off again to the mountains I go
To cleanse my spirit and soothe my soul,
To sit 'neath the arms of a big pine tree,
To humble my spirit, back down to my knees.

> *Oh, off to the mountains I go,*
> *Above the timberline, up by the snow,*
> *Where I can see more than I'll ever know,*
> *Off to the mountains, off to the mountains I go.*

Walk in the valley, golden aflame,
The aspens chatter with the wind and the rain.
Stand at the top of a cascading falls,
Stand there in wonder, stand there in awe.

> *Oh, off to the mountains I go,*
> *Above the timberline, up by the snow,*

Where I can see more than I'll ever know,
Off to the mountains, off to the mountains I go.

But it's not just the beauty or all that I see,
It's the love of the Creator rising in me.

Oh, off to the mountains I go,
Above the timberline, up by the snow,
Where I can see more than I'll ever know,
Off to the mountains, off to the mountains I go.

Off to the mountains, off to the mountains I go.

John M. Reichert

SEPTEMBER '94

This next song is easily one of my favorite songs, if not my most favorite. It was always my joy to end a concert with this song, especially if it was solo acoustic. I struggled with the last line, "I feel like You praise me too," but after consulting with many biblical scholars, I was assured that God can praise me too!

"When I Praise You"

Sometimes I sing a happy song,
Sometimes my tune is blue,
Even when the words of the song are sad,
I still lift my praise up to You.

> *When I praise You, praise You,*
> *My heart's lifted up with You.*
> *When I praise You, praise You,*
> *I feel like You praise me too.*

In those times when I don't think things are going right,
In those times when I just don't understand,
My security flows, knowing You're in control,
You hold it all in the palm of Your hand.

> *So, I praise You, praise You,*
> *My heart's lifted up with You.*

When I praise You, praise You,
I feel like You praise me too.

I will praise You, praise You, O Lord,
For You are worthy of praise.
I will praise You, praise You, O Lord,
Until the end, until the end, until the end of all of my days.

I will praise You, praise You,
And my heart's lifted up with You.
When I praise You, praise You,
I feel like You praise me too.
I feel like You praise me too.

John M. Reichert

NOVEMBER '94

The end of 1994 came with three Christmas-based songs. As I've already stated, I love the Christmas songs that God gives me.

"Peace and Joy"

Sing a song of Peace and Joy,
Goodwill to men of the earth.
Unite in chorus, sing with one voice,
Give praise for the Savior's birth.
Low in the manger, He was laid,
rejoice for His birth and give praise.
Joy, Joy, Joy to the world, the Savior is born today.

Bring gifts, treasures to lay at His feet,
Worship with humble hearts.
Like ox, cow, donkey, and sheep,
Nature performing her part.
The sounds of the angels announcing above
interpret the message to say,
Joy, Joy, Joy to the world, the Savior is born today.

> *Rejoice with the angels, glorious on high,*
> *Rejoice with the lowly, who stand at His side.*
> *Rejoice, rejoice, Immanuel, O rejoice.*

Sing a song of peace and joy,
Goodwill to men of the earth.
Unite in chorus, sing with one voice,
Give praise for the Savior's birth.
Low in the manger, He was laid,
fall on your knees and give praise,
Joy, Joy, Joy to the world, the Savior is born today.
Joy, Joy, Joy to the world, the Savior is born today.

It felt like God would give me songs so fast that it was almost impossible to get them on paper in a timely manner. I even bought a handheld recording device to put down lyrics and partial melodies to go back and finish later. I still have a binder full of partial songs.

"Prepare the Way"

Praise be to the Lord, the God of Israel
Redeemer of His own.
A horn raised up, salvation for us
From those who give us woe.

> *Prepare the way,*
> *O, child, prepare the way.*
> *Prepare the way,*
> *Prepare the way for the King of Kings.*

Unable to speak at the birth of my son,
Zechariah to be named,

Set loose was my tongue, "His name shall be John,
Baptizer be his fame."

> *Prepare the way,*
> *O, child, prepare the way.*
> *Prepare the way,*
> *Prepare the way for the King of Kings.*

To His people, give knowledge, forgiveness of sins
Because of our God's mercy, tender.
Shine the light in the darkness, the shadow of death,
Guide our feet on the path of surrender.

> *Prepare the way,*
> *O, child, prepare the way,*
> *Prepare the way,*
> *Prepare the way for the King of Kings.*

> *Prepare the way for the King of Kings.*

This is one of my wife Audrey's favorite songs, the third Christmas song in a row. I love the story of Simeon, a faithful man. Promised by God that his life would not end until he saw the promised one. My current pastor, Pastor Jack, says that God told him that he would not taste death, that he would be resurrected. I believe Pastor Jack is 87, so get ready, folks; it's coming soon!!

"Simeon"

He'd waited for so long, this man named Simeon,
To see Jehovah's Promised One, to see His Only Son.
So, he went to the temple, thinking this might be the day,
He'd seen the Star the prophets said would lead the way.

> *And if his dreams came true,*
> *If his prayers were answered too,*
> *Then he'd see more than he could ever hope for,*
> *He'd see the Lord.*

He was elated when they walked through the door,
A carpenter and his bride, but still, he wasn't sure.
Could this young child, this one so small,
Be the one to carry the burden and save us all?

> *O, Simeon, O, Righteous man, O, man devout!*
> *Why is it now that you show such doubt?*
> *Wasn't it promised to you that before you died*
> *You'd see the light of revelation, Messiah, the Christ?*

Simeon took the child, burst out in smile, and praised God;
Never before, such joy, in all the years, that he walked this sod.
"I've seen salvation, Lord, dismiss me if You please,
My life's been filled to overflowing; Your servant goes in peace."

> *And his dreams came true,*
> *His prayers were answered too.*
> *He held in his arms all his dreams and more—*
> *Simeon held the Lord.*
>
> *Yes, Simeon held the Lord.*

John M. Reichert

JANUARY '95

There are all kinds of sermons about Abraham and how he was willing to sacrifice his son Isaac. God saw that this was good, and all nations were blessed because of Abraham's willingness to do what God wanted. But have you ever looked at it through Isaac's eyes. Here is a 15-17-year-old lad whose dad is taking him to the mountains to sacrifice. It was several days' journey; you think Isaac had questions? I'm sure he did. There were no matches or lighters back then, so guess who got to carry the wood and the fire?

"Carry the Fire"

Carry the fire, carry the fire,
Fill up your heart with holy desire
And carry the fire.

Carry the flame, carry the flame,
Garment your life with His Holy Name
And carry the flame.

> *Like Isaac for Abraham, a sacrifice made,*
> *Though they had no perfect lamb, the Lord knew a way.*
> *But the offering meant not so much as the test of the truth,*
> *God needed to know if to the mountain they'd go and carry it through.*

Would you carry the wood? Would you carry the wood
Not knowing the price of doing the good?
Would you carry the wood?

> *Like Isaac for Abraham, a sacrifice made,*
> *Though they had no perfect lamb, the Lord knew a way.*
> *But the offering meant not so much as the test of the truth,*
> *God needed to know if to the mountain they'd go and carry*
>   *it through.*

Carry the light, carry the light,
Be prepared through His word to do what is right
And carry the light.

Carry the fire, carry the fire,
Fill up your heart with holy desire; Carry the fire.
Fill all your hopes with holy desires and carry the fire.

John M. Reichert

MARCH '95

I was talking with the guys in Crooked Nail about how we could get kids more involved at our concerts at churches. And BAM! God gave me a sing-along song for kids. We'd bring all the kids up front and nervously give them one or two of our microphones. Then they were instructed that anytime they heard the word "animals," they were to make all kinds of animal sounds, barking, mooing, oinking, or whatever their preference was. Sometimes it got out of control, as you can imagine! But it sure was fun!!!

"Wooden Zoo"

Open the spicket, pull out the plug,
Let the waters flow, bring on the flood.
Gather up the animals, two by two,
Lock them all up in a wooden zoo.

Noah was a righteous man, He walked with God.
God said, "Noah, there's sin in this land, and I'm going to have to destroy this sod."
"Noah, build me a big ol' boat out of gopher wood, so it will float."
"Gather up some animals and gather some hay,
'cause you're going to be locked up for many a day."

> Open the spicket, pull out the plug,
> Let the waters flow, bring on the flood.
> Gather up the animals, two by two,
> Lock them all up in a wooden zoo.

300 cubits long and 50 cubits wide, 300 cubits long and 30 cubits high.
A big ol' boat and a gray-haired old man are sure a funny site in a desert land.
Noah hammered day and night; Noah hammered with all his might,
Noah knew the plans God had in mind…Worldwide…High tide.

> Open the spicket, pull out the plug,
> Let the waters flow, bring on the flood.
> Gather up the animals, two by two,
> Lock them all up in a wooden zoo.

Well, the animals were loaded, and the rain started falling—
That's when the neighbors all came a calling.
"Noah," they cried, "Noah, let us in"
But God had locked them out because of their sin, then He…

> Opened the spicket, pulled out the plug,
> Let the waters flow, brought on the flood.
> Gathered up the animals, two by two,
> Locked them all up in a wooden zoo.

> Moral of the story, tell your sons and daughters
> God can make it rain longer than you can tread the water when He…

John M. Reichert

Opens the spicket, pulls out the plug,
Let the waters flow, brings on the flood.
Gathers up the animals, two by two,
Locks them all up in a wooden zoo.

God gave me this next song to write for a friend's wedding. I have had a couple of people sing this at weddings, and a friend, who is a DJ, told me he plays it at every wedding reception he does.

I couldn't be more blessed.

"Hand In Hand"

Guide us as we walk hand in hand;
Lead us as today we take our stand.
Help us when it seems we can't decide;
Heal us when we hurt down deep inside.

Teach us when it seems there's no way out;
Strengthen us if our faith should show some doubt.
Hear us when we lift our prayers to You;
Love us when we do the things we do.

> *Hand in hand, we start today together;*
> *Hand in hand, we're asking for Your love.*
> *In Your sight, we pledge our love forever,*
> *And we know things work out as You plan If we follow*
>   *You—Hand in Hand.*

Warm us when our hearts are feeling cold;
Comfort us, as our days are growing old.
Keep us in the shelter of Your hand;
Guide us as we walk Hand in Hand.

> *Hand in hand, we start today together;*
> *Hand in hand, we're asking for Your love.*
> *In Your sight, we pledge our love forever,*
> *And we know things work out as You plan If we follow*
>   *You—Hand in Hand.*

> *And we know things work out as You plan*
> *When we follow You Hand in Hand.*

John M. Reichert

APRIL '95

Sometimes I get so frustrated with God. And I believe it's okay to tell Him so. I also think you should have a scripture handy to quote back to God to let Him know where you are coming from! I also know that every time I have been in a state of weakness, He has made me strong.

Second Corinthians 12:10 (KJV) says, "Therefore, I take pleasure in infirmities, in reproaches, in necessities, in persecutions, in distress for Christ's sake: for when I am weak, then I am strong."

"When I Am Weak"

Lord, please forgive me again; today
I lost my patience with You.
It seems that lately, things aren't going my way,
And I've forgotten what to do.

> *Maybe I should spend more time down on my knees;*
> *Maybe the words I hid in my heart are just what I need.*

> *When I am weak, You make me strong.*
> *When it seems the roads too long, You help me carry on.*
> *When I feel the load is much, too much to bear,*
> *When I am weak, when I am weak,*
> *When I am weak, Lord You are there.*

Lately, it's warmer; it seems a little brighter,
Sometimes, the sun comes shining through,
Even the journey feels a little lighter,
Lord, I owe it all to You.

> *When I am weak, You make me strong.*
> *When it seems the roads too long, You help me carry on.*
> *When I feel the load is much, too much to bear,*
> *When I am weak, when I am weak,*
>
> *When I am weak, Lord, You still care. When I am weak,*
>   *Lord, You are there.*

John M. Reichert

JUNE '95

Another praise song to my Lord and Savior.

"Lift Up Your Voice"

Lift up your voice to the Lord,
Lift up your voice to the Son of our God.
Sing adulation, Hope of Salvation,
Sing 'til the whole world has heard.
Lift up your voice to the Lord.

Lift up your hands to the King,
Lift up your hands to the Son of our God.
Work never tiring, always desiring,
Humbly your services bring.
Lift up your hands to the King.

> *Lift up your voice,*
> *Lift up your hands,*
> *Lift up your life*
> *To the Lord of the lands.*

Lift up your life to the Lord,
Lift up your life to the Lamb of our God.
Full in His favor, living forever,
Glory to God's Holy word.
Lift up your life to the Lord.

Sing adulation, Hope of Salvation,
Glory to God's Holy Word.
Lift up your voice to the Lord.
Lift up your voice to the Lord.

John M. Reichert

JULY '95

This next song came to me as a friend of mine was going through a really tough time. I guess the Beatles said it too, "All you need is love," but I'm not sure they knew Jesus!

"Love Will See You Through"

Nobody said it would be easy,
That you could have your cake and eat it too.
Nobody said the sun would still be shining
When the day is through.

Nobody said the path is level,
That uphill climbs would never be in your way.
Nobody said a little rain would not fall
On your parade.

> *Love will see you through,*
> *Love will see you through.*
> *As you navigate the passageways life will throw at you,*
> *God's love will see you through.*

Nobody said it would be easy,
That everything would work out just as you planned.
Nobody said that you should carry it through
Without a helping hand.

Nobody said there are no questions
That some days answers seem to not come at all.
Nobody said that you would always be ready
For the Fall.

> *Love will see you through,*
> *Love will see you through.*
> *As you navigate the passageways life will throw at you,*
> *God's love will see you through.*

There will be times that you think He does not care;
He is there, walking beside you.
There will be times that are filled with deep despair;
He is a friend, and He will guide you.

Nobody said there is no sorrow
That would not follow you wherever you go.
Nobody said you can't have pain in your heart
And peace in your soul.

> *Love will see you through,*
> *Love will see you through.*
> *As you navigate the passageways life will throw at you,*
> *God's love will see you through.*

Have you ever read the Song of Songs, also known as the Song of Solomon? This is a very steamy book in the Bible. A book of love…July 1995 song "Friends and Lovers." This is my attempt at being steamy. It is not about anyone in particular but a reflection of Solomon.

"Friends and Lovers"

He says he loves her, loves her hair,
He thinks about her when he is not there.
He loves her painted lips of ruby red,
He says he'll love her 'til the day he is dead.

She says she loves him, arms so strong,
She thinks about him all day long.
She knows his duties take him far from home,
Still, she can't wait 'til she can have him alone.

> *Friends and lovers, king and queen,*
> *Friends and lovers, such an eloquent thing.*
> *Each one trying hard to lift up the other,*
> *They are friends, friends, and lovers.*

She says she loves his eyes, black-like pearls,
He says he loves her perfumed smell of myrrh.
He could give her gold and diamonds, jewels and furs,
She says she needs his touch to feel secure.

> *Friends and lovers, king and queen,*
> *Friends and lovers, such an eloquent thing.*
> *Each one trying hard to lift up the other,*
> *They are friends, friends, and lovers.*

He could have chosen any other maiden,
She only wanted this one king.
Passion burns and never has faded,
All they think about is just one thing.

He says he loves her, says he cares,
He thinks about her when he is not there.

She thinks about him all day long,
And she can't wait 'til she can have him alone.

> *Friends and lovers, king and queen,*
> *Friends and lovers, such an eloquent thing.*
> *Each one trying hard to lift up the other,*
> *They are friends, friends, and lovers.*

John M. Reichert

AUGUST '95

Mark 16:15–16 (KJV) says, "And he said unto them, go ye into all the world, and preach the gospel to every creature. He that believeth and is baptized shall be saved; but he that believeth not shall be damned."

"Let It Out"

So many people who have not heard
The special treasure in God's Word.
They live their lives on the dying edge;
Some of these people you call friends.

> *Do you want to see them throw it away?*
> *Do you want to see them end it this way?*

> *Let it out, oh, let them see*
> *What Jesus has done for you and me.*
> *Get under that bush and bring out the light,*
> *Shine the love of Jesus,*
> *Shine it so bright*
> *And let it out.*

They walk around in a great big haze,
They are wandering day to day.
They need something solid to hold on to,
That piece of the Rock is me and you, so...

*Let it out, oh, let them see
What Jesus has done for you and me.
Get under that bush and bring out the light,
Shine the love of Jesus,
Shine it so bright
And let it out.*

*Let it out and bring them in;
Let it out and bring them in.*

SEPTEMBER '95

My King, my Messiah, and my Lord deserves nothing but all my praise and worship. I heard someone once say that an Alleluia is worth 10,000 Hallelujahs!

"Alleluia"

Alleluia, Alleluia, Alleluia to the King,
Alleluia, Alleluia, Alleluia to the King.
Alleluia, Alleluia, Alleluias we sing,
Alleluia, Alleluia, Alleluia to the King.

Come Messiah, come Messiah, come Messiah, come again,
Come Messiah, come Messiah, come Messiah, come again.
Alleluia, Alleluia, Alleluia, praise His name,
Come Messiah, come Messiah, come Messiah, come again.

Live forever, live forever, live forever, King of Kings,
Live forever, live forever, live forever, King of Kings.
Alleluia, Alleluia, Alleluia to the King,
Live forever, live forever, live forever, King of Kings.

Alleluia, Alleluia, Alleluia to the King,
Alleluia, Come Messiah, Life forever, King of Kings.
Alleluia, Alleluia, Alleluia to the King,
Alleluia, Alleluia, Alleluia to the King.

OCTOBER '95

Our Christian band had been playing together for a few years, but we never had a "name" for the band. My brother-in-law and I were talking one day, and he said, "You should write a song about a guy who works at a lumber yard straightening bent nails so that they can be used again." I think my brother-in-law had that job at one time. I thought it was an interesting idea for a song and prayed God would give me a song like this. It even became our band name.

"Crooked Nail"

When I was a boy, I used to work for a carpenter;
The days were long and hard.
I remember when he told me to go down
To the local lumberyard.

Ask the man if you can go out back
And pick up all the crooked nails.
Fill a bucket, boy, and bring them back;
By the way, you're doing well.

A crooked nail is no good to us;
It must be true and straight.
Pick up a hammer, boy, and pound out the bends;
It'll probably take all day.

All you need is a little patience,
A firm and gentle hand.
Soon you'll see that all the crooked nails
Can be used again.

That was years ago, and now I see
What the carpenter had meant.
All those crooked nails were just like me
In God's eternal plan.

All it took was His gentle touch
To take the bend from me.
You see, the little boy was Jesus,
And the crooked nail was me.

> *Crooked nail bent and ugly, it's no good to use, you see.*
> *Crooked nail, oh the crooked nail was me, was me,*
> *I am the crooked nail.*

DECEMBER '95

I saw a Bob Ross program on TV. Wonderful! I thought he was amazing. So, I bought a "Bob Ross" starter set and began my painting endeavors. I even got my son, Zachary, to paint a picture with me.

His first attempt at age thirteen, I thought, was marvelous. Zach decided to take his painting for an art class at school. The disappointment he felt when his teacher told him that he couldn't have painted that picture must have been tremendous. I wish he would take it up again; it's one of his hidden talents.

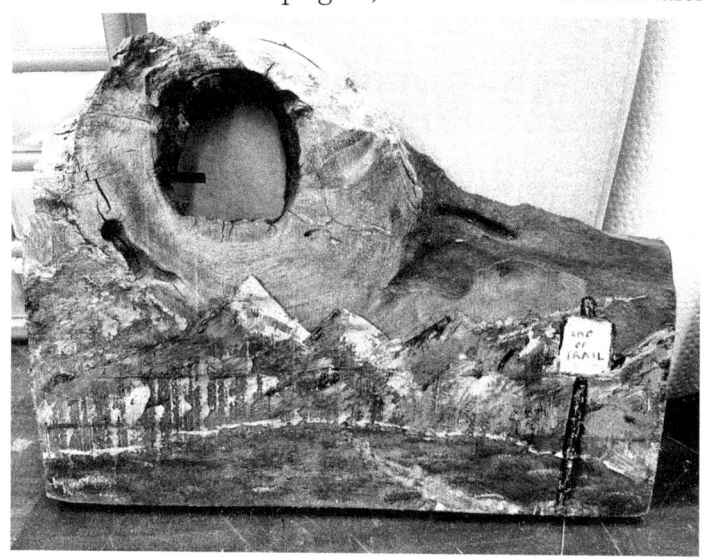

John M. Reichert

This is one I painted for Zach of a trip we took to the Badlands together, to a place called "Hole-in-the-Wall." This was painted on a piece of black walnut.

When Zach was thirteen, we were headed to soccer practice, and we had to go up over Toll Road. This gave an unobstructed view to the west. It was evening, and the sun was starting to get lower in the sky. The colors were outstanding, and Zach's comment to me was. "Did God paint the sky?"

My answer: "Yes, He did, Zach. Yes, He did!!"

"Paint the Sky"

A little child, a great big world, so much to understand,
A little wild, like the wind that whirls—against it, he makes his stand.
But somewhere in that restless heart is a child beyond his days;
When he looks out at the western sky, and then you hear him say:

> *"Only God can make the wind blow,*
> *Only God can make the sky snow.*
> *Only God can keep the rivers from running to the sea,*
> *Only God can paint the sky for you and me."*

A teenage boy, the same big world, life is changing so fast,
Don't need no toys; it's sports and girls. How long will these moments last?
Somewhere deep inside his soul is a spark that keeps your faith
When he looks up from his study books, and you think you hear him say:

> *"Only God controls the sunshine,*
> *Only God can move the stars in time.*

Only God can keep the ocean from rolling to the shore,
Only God can give His love, then give it even more."

Maybe it's true what they say,
From the mouth of babes,
There's a little bit of wisdom in everything they say.

Only God can make the wind blow,
Only God can make the sky snow.
Only God can keep the rivers from running to the sea,
Only God can paint the sky for you and me.

JANUARY '96

I really dislike bullies. I was a skinny kid growing up. Always the shortest, the smallest, and the slowest. I think in the fourth grade, I was forty-eight pounds and forty-eight inches tall—not something to be proud of. Seems like there was always someone on the playground pushing you around. One time in the fifth grade, at recess, I was just walking across the play field, and all of a sudden, someone jumped me from behind. Immediately I was on the ground, and the person was punching me. I was getting ready to punch back when I realized it was a girl. Fifth grade, whooped by a girl. Bullies!

"Is It Now?"

Recess, here he comes again,
across the playground;
Said, "Hey, kid, I'm going to smash your face in,
Lay you flat out on the ground."

I felt like running 'til I remembered
what my Sunday school teacher said,
"To beat your enemy, turn your cheek,
heap burning coals on his head."

  Is it now that I reach to hold Your hand?
  That I rise to take a stand?

> That I show my faith and trust in You?
> Is it now that I close my eyes and pray?
> That You lead me all the way?
> That Your guiding light comes shining through, is it now?

Another bully backed against the wall,
this one you can't see.
Temptation, it's hard to make the call—
Right or wrong, what will it be?

I feel like running,
but there's nowhere to go to get away,
I won the last time, but it wasn't easy—
hope I remember the way.

> Is it now that I reach to hold Your hand?
> That I finally understand?
> That You always, always care for me?
> Is it now that I close my eyes to pray?
> Know You're with me all the way?
> That You always have been there for me, is it now?

> Any time's the right time to call upon the Lord,
> Any day or nighttime, you're surely to be heard.

> Is it now that I reach to hold Your hand?
> That I finally understand?
> That I show my faith and trust in You?
> Is it now that I close my eyes to pray?
> That You drive the dark away?
> That Your guiding light comes shining through, is it now?

John M. Reichert

One of my favorite hymns is Lord Lift Me Up and Let Me Stand by Johnson Oatman, Jr; 1898. The last verse says, "I want to scale the utmost height, and catch a gleam of glory bright; but still I'll pray till heaven I've found, Lord plant my feet on higher ground." I believe Mr. Oatman must have loved the mountains as much as I. This is my version of "Higher Ground."

"Higher Ground"

"Lord, lift me up and let me stand
by faith in Thy almighty hand.
A higher plane that I have found,
Lord, plant my feet on higher ground."

When storm clouds gather low and you hear thunder roll,
Lightning flashes all around.
Before the coming flood, reach for the hand of love and pray,
"Lord, lift me up to higher ground."

> *Higher Ground, Higher Ground,*
> *Lord, set my feet on higher ground;*
> *Higher Ground, Higher Ground,*
> *Lord, lift me up to higher ground.*

When your darkest night swallows all the light
And you feel that you may drown,
There is a place that's right, where the light is bright—
It is a place of higher ground.

> *Higher Ground, Higher Ground,*
> *Lord, set my feet on higher ground,*
> *Higher Ground, Higher Ground,*
> *Lord, lift me up to higher ground.*

From the height of life to the sacrifice,
One man, one death, no sound.
The stone rolled away, risen on that day,
Risen to a place of higher ground.

> *Higher Ground, Higher Ground,*
> *Lord, set my feet on higher ground,*
> *Higher Ground, Higher Ground,*
> *Lord, lift me up to higher ground.*

John M. Reichert

FEBRUARY '96

In February 1996, I wrote a tribute to Dan Fogelberg. He has long been a favorite singer, songwriter, and lyricist. Unless you know a lot of Dan's songs, this might not mean anything to you.

"Of Songs, Of Souls, Of Hearts"

I saw her smile and raise her glass and drink a toast to you at last
And find the bottle hidden high, unfold the paper, read the lines.
I saw the yellows and the grays of winter skies so far away,
Where love had left untended fires and walked away from heart's desires.

> *I sailed on oceans full of life, I felt the Minstrel fall and rise,*
> *I climbed with you through mountain snows to satisfy the need to know.*
> *You are a poet, you are a craftsman of sorts,*
> *A sculpture of art, painter of songs, of souls, of hearts.*

I sometimes took the long way home, who understands the comes and goes,
The fear and joy in pilgrims' faith that humble hearts anticipate.
It's always hard to make love stay, the love we have is hard to say,
Through stolen moments, we have sailed, some through heaven, some through hell.

I've been the last to know and see what others find hard to believe,
A patient love, a love that's sound, can take you to a higher ground.
You are a poet, you are a craftsman of sorts,
A sculpture of art, painter of songs, of souls, of hearts.

You were right to say love more; too soon, they pass eternal doors.
Forefathers who before us go, a love like this, to us they show.
I cried with you when in decline and thought of loves you brought to mind,
I knelt and touched your kindred steps on spirit trails where we both wept.

We live our lives in worlds of men, not make believe of straw and tin,
And since you asked, you need to know you left your brush marks on my soul.
You are a poet, you are a craftsman of sorts,
A sculpture of art, painter of songs, of souls, of hearts.

John M. Reichert

APRIL '96

Poor Nicodemus, he couldn't understand how a grown man could be born again into his mother's womb. Jesus related to Nicodemus that he could see the effects of the wind but not the wind itself; and that was like being born of the Spirit. Being born again is by faith, you can't see it or touch it, like the wind. The story of Nicodemus gives us one of the greatest verses in all the Bible. John 3:16 (KJV): "For God so loved the world that he gave His only begotten Son, that whosoever believeth in Him should not perish, but have everlasting life".

"Nicodemus"

You see the sun rise, see the stars rise,
You see the rain fall down.
You see the hawk fly, hear a baby cry,
You see the sky and ground.

You don't know what to do with something that you can't see,
You don't know what to do with someone quite like Me.

> *O, Nicodemus, from where does the wind blow?*
> *O, Nicodemus, to where does that wind go?*
> *You hear its sound, but you can't see it;*
> *Still, Nicodemus, you believe it.*

> *If you believe in the wind, you can believe forgiveness of sins,*
> *O, Nicodemus.*

You see the boats sail, you see the sky hail,
You see the night and day.
You see the stone walls, walked in palace halls,
You see the marketplace.

But you don't know what to do with the message that you received,
You don't know on which heavenly things you must believe.

> *O, Nicodemus, from where does the wind blow?*
> *O, Nicodemus, to where does that wind go?*
> *You hear its sound, but you can't see it;*
> *Still, Nicodemus, you believe it.*
> *If you believe in the wind, you can believe forgiveness of sins,*
> *O, Nicodemus.*

Can't see the wind, but you can hear it,
Born of water and born of the Spirit.

> *O, Nicodemus, from where does the wind blow?*
> *O, Nicodemus, to where does that wind go?*
> *You hear its sound, but you can't see it;*
> *Still, Nicodemus, you believe it.*
> *If you believe in the wind, you can believe forgiveness of sins,*
> *O, Nicodemus.*

John M. Reichert

Crooked Nail would close with the next song many times. We would have the audience stand up and clap along with the song. After it was over, we would thank the crowd for a standing ovation. Bad humor, but it worked!!

"Keep the Faith"

Keep the faith, hold on strong;
you know He's coming back, it won't be long,
Then we will all join together,
giving praise and honor to our Savior.

> *Oh, Oh, Oh, praise to our Savior;*
> *Oh, Oh, Oh, praise to our Savior.*

And you know it will be great if we all just keep the faith.

Keep the faith, keep on working; the hands of time,
you know, they keep on turning.
It won't be long until we all will sing
praise and honor to the King of Kings.

> *Oh, Oh, Oh, sing for the King;*
> *Oh, Oh, Oh, sing for the King.*

Yes, we know it will be great if we all just keep the faith.

Keep the faith, keep a smile;
we've read the end of the story, there's no more trials;
It won't be long until we fall upon our knees
and worship God the Father for eternity.

> *Oh, Oh, Oh, for eternity;*
> *Oh, Oh, Oh, for eternity.*

Yes, we know it will be great, and we all anticipate,
Well, you know we just can't wait, so we try to keep the faith.

    Oh, Oh, Oh, keep the faith;
    Oh, Oh, Oh, keep the faith.

JUNE '96

I've read that the best strategic location in a battle is to fight from a higher vantage point. From a hill, if you will. THE Battle was won on a hill.

"Once Upon a Hill"

Once upon a hill, there stood a man,
The battle raged around him; he lifted up his hands.
It gave the fighting people hope a victory be revealed,
They fought for land God gave to them, once upon a hill.

Once upon a hill, there stood a man,
Surrounded by his enemy, a jawbone in his hand.
They story is told how he swung the bone, and a thousand men were killed;
He fought the battle of the Lord, once upon a hill.

>   *Upon a hill is where God shows to you and me*
>   *Miracle upon miracle, there for all to see.*

Once upon a hill, there stood a man,
Five loaves of bread and two small fish were placed within His hands.
He fed the thousands listening as He spoke His Father's will
Just outside of Galilee, once upon a hill.

Upon a hill is where God shows to you and me
Miracle upon miracle, there for all to see.

Once upon a hill, there hung a man,
Forsaken by His Father, the nails had pierced His hands.
He paid the cost upon the cross, a kingdom He would fill
By giving all, He had for all, once upon a hill.

By dying once, He died for all, once upon a hill.

John M. Reichert

JULY '96

Do you have someone to lean on in a time of need? I'm not talking about Jesus, who we should always lean on, but someone who will pray with you and take you and your trials boldly before the throne of God. The Bible says wherever two or more are gathered together, Jesus will be there also. There are troubling times coming as we are in the final days. Stand in unity; stand together!

"Stand Together"

There's a dark night coming before the brightest day,
It's coming from the east and west and north and south, they say.
Is there someone you can lean on should you stumble, should you fall?
Is there someone whose name you can call?

There's a cold wind blowing, and the time is getting short,
The path keeps heading toward the kingdom; there's no thoughts of getting off.
Is there someone who will help you, someone to see you through?
Is there someone you can trust to say to you?

> *We will stand together,*
> *We will pray for one another,*
> *And on that great day,*

> *Inside the pearly gates,*
> *We will hear the Savior say, forever,*
> *"Come stand together."*

The master of evil will do all that he can
To stop your daily progress toward the promised land.
Find support, find some hope, and find yourself a friend
Who will walk the journey with you to the end.

> *We will stand together,*
> *We will pray for one another,*
> *And on that great day,*
> *Inside the pearly gates,*
> *We will hear the Savior say, forever,*
> *"Come stand together."*

John M. Reichert

AUGUST '96

In August 1996, God gave me the following lyrics for a song, but no music. He does that occasionally, and that's okay. His ways are not my ways!!

"People On the Street"

Are the people on the street smiling when you meet?
Do they know your Jesus?

Do they sing a happy song? Do they sing it all day long?
Do they know your Jesus?

Do they know He loves and cares for them
As He holds them in His hands?

Are the people on the street smiling as you meet?
Do they know your Jesus?

Are the people on the street crying when you meet?
Are they lost and lonely?

Is there darkness in their soul? Is there someone they should know?
Are they lost and lonely?

Have you told them that He died for them?
Have you told them that He cares?

Are the people on the street crying as you meet?
Are they lost and lonely?

Tell them all how much He loves them;
Tell them all how much He cares.

Tell the people on the street, tell the people when you meet,
Tell the people on the street about Jesus.

John M. Reichert

SEPTEMBER '96

Here's a weird thing: God provided me with lyrics but no music for two months in a row. I always thought that maybe there was someone out there to whom God gave music but no lyrics.

He should bring us together!

"Let It Shine"

*Even though the darkness of the world keeps closing in on me
and fights against my will,
I stand ready with the fire of God; down deep inside of me,
my tinderbox is filled.*

*Those of us who carry fire endeavor now to persevere;
we seek the strength to carry on.
Those of us who carry fire, dispel the dark and gather near;
side by side, we sing our song.*

> *Let it shine, let it shine, let it shine, until the end of time,
> Let it shine, let it shine, let it shine, O this little light of
> mine.*

*Evil like a black hole pulling all around it deep inside;
even light cannot escape,
Spinning, twisting, pulling, grabbing, all the light it tries to hide
inside its twisted face.*

Those of us who carry fire must raise the torch and hold it high to light the path for all to see.
Those of us who carry fire must pass the torch and spread the light, help more to believe.

> *Let it shine, let it shine, let it shine, until the end of time,*
> *Let it shine, let it shine, let it shine, O this little light of mine.*

Someone's standing in the shadow, lost
They face the night; there is no day
Won't you share the light of Jesus' cross,
Help them find the Way?

> *Let it shine, let it shine, let it shine, until the end of time,*
> *Let it shine, let it shine, let it shine, O this little light of mine.*

John M. Reichert

OCTOBER '96

One of Crooked Nail's members played keyboards and synthesizers for the band. He had a gazillion different sounds on his board. This next song started with the sound of the wind blowing. The kind of wind that blows through pine trees in the mountains. As the song evolved, the sound of thunder could be heard. And sometimes, you could get an audience member to participate and flash the lights on and off, in the sanctuary, for lightning.

"Thunder and Lightning"

On the cross, King of Kings,
Satan jeers, the angels sing.
On the cross, the victory,
Death is dead, eternally.

On a hill, lightning strikes,
The day becomes as dark as night.
On a hill, thunders rolls;
The Savior dies to save my soul.

>   *On a hill, the world can see,*
>   *On the skull, Golgotha's tree.*
>   *Where lightnings flash and thunder rolls;*
>   *The Savior dies to save my soul.*

On the Rock, foundation laid,
The church is built, is built to stay.
On the Rock, the corner stone,
The kingdom walls, the chosen's home.

> *On the Rock, on Salem's hill,*
> *The temple mount, the church is filled.*
> *The lightnings flash, and thunder rolls;*
> *There is a place to rest my soul.*

From the heavens, lightning strikes,
The day becomes the brightest light.
From the heavens, thunder rolls;
The Savior comes to take me home.

> *On a hill, the world can see,*
> *On the skull, Golgotha's tree.*
> *Where lightnings flash and thunder rolls,*
> *The Savior comes to take my soul.*

John M. Reichert

NOVEMBER '96

One of my favorite songs that God gave me!! A Christmas song about the star through the eyes of the wisemen.

"The Star"

We spotted it shining over the mountains,
A Star that would guide us out of the east.
We knew it was coming; the prophets had told us,
"Go into Judea, and there you will see a King of Peace."

> We traveled all day; we traveled all night,
> The star never left us; it stayed in our sight.
> We trusted it's leading, our course we set true,
> We knew that to follow the star would bring us to You.

We spotted it shining over the city,
A jewel of the valley, old Bethlehem.
We followed its lighting into the city,
We knew we would find, in a matter of time, God's only Lamb.

> We traveled all day; we traveled all night,
> The star never left us; it stayed in our sight.
> We trusted it's leading, our course we set true,
> We knew that to follow the star would bring us to You.

We spotted it shining over the rooftop,
Where He was dwelling as a young boy.
We entered the building, where the star stopped,
And there in that place, to look on His face, filled us with joy.

    So, we gave Him our gold that we held in our purse,
    We gave Him our frankincense, gave Him our myrrh.
    We lay at His feet all the gifts that we bring,
    Then we fell to our faces to worship the King.

    We traveled all day; we traveled all night,
    The star never left us; it stayed in our sight.
    We trusted it's leading, our course we set true,
    We knew that to follow the star would bring us to You.

John M. Reichert

JANUARY '97

Sometimes God gives you a song that you just love. This is one of those songs. Sometimes the melody comes first, then the lyrics; sometimes, it is vise-a-versa. On this occasion, it happened at the same time.

"Walk Across the Desert"

Well, I'm backed up against some trouble, can't always find my way out,
It's easy to forget how much He loves you when you're underneath the shadow of doubt.
I know He leads me, by the hand, across the river Jordan, to the Promised Land.

> *I will walk across the desert, eat manna from the sky,*
> *I will drop down on my knees and worship God on high.*
> *Before I walk out of this building, I'll tell everyone I see,*
> *When I walk across the desert, my God, He walks with me.*

There are good times, there are bad, can't always tell them apart,
But I know that all the good times that I have come falling from my God and Savior's heart.
I know He's with me all the way; I know He wouldn't have it any other way.

I will walk across the desert, eat manna from the sky,
I will drop down on my knees and worship God on high.
Before I walk out of this building, I'll tell everyone I see,
When I walk across the desert, my God, He walks with me.

He's always standing there waiting on me,
He's my heart's desire.
He's my protector when my back's against the sea,
He's my pillar of fire.

I will walk across the desert, eat manna from the sky,
I will drop down on my knees and worship God on high.
Before I walk out of this building, I'll tell everyone I see,
When I walk across the desert, my God, He walks with me.

When I walk across the desert, my God, He walks with me.

MARCH '97

I have always been generous with the band and allowed each player to add their own "feel" to the song. I have heard that some artists are very strict and have perfectionistic rule over how the song is put together. I rarely do that unless it is a blues tune and somebody is trying to play disco during it. This is another blues tune God gave me.

"All God's People"

All God's people want to clap their hands,
all God's people want to clap their hands.
All God's people want to clap their hands;
they want to clap their hands.

All God's people want to join hands and sing,
all God's people want to join hands and sing.
All God's people want to join hands and sing;
they want to sing unto the Lord

> *All God's people, all God's people,*
> *All God's people, they want to sing unto the Lord.*

All God's people want to stand up and shout,
all God's people want to stand up and shout.
All God's people want to stand up and shout;
they want to shout unto the Lord.

> *All God's people, all God's people,*
> *All God's people, they want to shout unto the Lord.*

All God's people want to kneel and pray,
all God's people want to kneel and pray.
All God's people want to kneel and pray;
they want to pray unto the Lord.

All God's people want to lift up their praise,
all God's people want to lift up their praise.
All God's people want to lift up their praise,
lift up their praise unto the Lord.

> *All God's people, all God's people,*
> *All God's people singing praises to the Lord.*

All God's people want to stand up and shout,
all God's people want to stand up and shout.
All God's people want to stand up and shout;
they want to shout unto the Lord.

They want to shout unto the Lord.

In Luke 1:45–55 (KJV), the Blessed Mother Mary, after the angel of God came to her to tell her she would be the mother of the Messiah, goes to Elisabeth's house. Elisabeth, who is carrying John the Baptist in her womb, feels the baby leap when Mary gives her salutation. Mary then, in verse 46, goes into her canticle.

"Mary's Song"

My soul glorifies the Lord, my spirit rejoices in the Savior,
My soul glorifies the Lord, my spirit rejoices in the Savior.

> *My God is mindful of me;*
> *Holy is His Name.*
> *With mighty arms and deeds,*
> *He has lifted up His humble servant's name.*

My soul glorifies the Lord, my spirit rejoices in the Savior,
My soul glorifies the Lord, my spirit rejoices in the Savior.

> *He has brought down the rulers from their thrones,*
> *He has filled the hungry,*
> *He has settled the restless in their home,*
> *He has remembered to be merciful forever.*

> *My God is mindful of me;*
> *Holy is His Name.*
> *With mighty arms and deeds,*
> *He has lifted up His humble servant's name.*

My soul glorifies the Lord, my spirit rejoices in the Savior,
My soul glorifies the Lord, my spirit rejoices in the Savior.

My spirit rejoices in, my spirit rejoices in,
My spirit rejoices in the Lord.

MAY '97

Fifty years after high school choir, I had the pleasure of getting together with many of my choir mates and performing a song we performed in high school. It was directed by our former choir director, Don Dowdy. Don has gone on to be with Jesus, but he sure left his mark on many choir students. During this program, I was blessed with the opportunity to perform one of the songs God has given me.

"Light of Jesus"

As I journey up and down this kingdom road,
there are people that I meet,
Some are searching, some are walking all alone,
and it's Jesus that they seek.

As I look into the eyes of desperation,
an empty darkness can be seen,
I can see no hope of reconciliation;
there's no faith on which they lean.

They are looking for the answers
to the questions that they pose,
They are looking for direction;
they don't know which way to go.

> *Let the light of Jesus shine today,*
> *shine for all the world to see,*
> *Let the light of Jesus light their way;*
> *let it shine through you and me.*

As they wander through this dark and evil time,
they are looking for a friend.
They are reaching for whatever they can find;
they are fearful of the end.

They are looking for an anchor
to keep their souls from drifting more,
They are looking for the lighthouse
that will guide them to the shore.

> *Let the light of Jesus shine today,*
> *shine for all the world to see;*
> *Let the light of Jesus light their way,*
> *let it shine through you and me.*

> *Let the light of Jesus shine today,*
> *shine for all the world to see;*
> *Let the light of Jesus light their way,*
> *let it shine through you and me.*

JULY '97

This next song had something unique for an introduction. Crooked Nail was fortunate to have multiple bass players. They took the duties of performing a double bass intro to "Dance." Only wish you could hear it!! Sorry!!

"Dance"

Dance, Dance in celebration,
Dance with all the nations,
Dance before the King.
Dance, Dance in revelation,
Dance in exaltation,
Dance before the King.

> *For He is worthy to be honored.*
> *He is worthy to be praised.*
> *He is the one who gave up His Life*
> *That all men might be saved.*

Sing, lift your voice with praises,
sing through all the ages,
Sing before the King.
Sing, for the coming kingdom,
Sing in honor of the One,
Sing before the King

John M. Reichert

> For He is worthy to be honored.
> He is worthy to be praised.
> He is the one who died on the cross
> That all men might be saved.
>
> For He is worthy to be honored.
> He is worthy to be praised.
> He is the one who gave up His Life
> That all men might be saved.

Shout, shout out the victory,
defeat of the enemy,
shout before the King.
Shout so mountain and river hear,
so the enemy shakes with fear,
shout before the King.

> For He is worthy to be honored.
> He is worthy to be praised.
> He is the one who rose from the dead
> That all men might be saved.

SEPTEMBER '97

There is only one source, our Lord. Money can't buy it, promotions can't evaluate you to the level, and relationships will usually, at some point, let you down. But what a friend we have in Jesus!!

"Look to the Lord"

When you're looking for hope, look to the Lord.
When you're looking for peace, look to the Lord.
When you're looking for the steps to take as you're walking day to day,
When you're looking for the light that drives the darkness all away,
Look to the Lord.

When you're looking for strength, look to the Lord.
When you're looking for power, look to the Lord.
When you're looking for a hand to guide your walk along the road,
When you're looking for the kind of friend that makes a miracle,
Look to the Lord.

When you're looking all around you and you feel you don't fit in,
When you're feeling lost and lonely and the world is closing in,
There is one who stands beside you, just waiting for your call;
Look to the Lord.

John M. Reichert

When you're looking for truth, look to the Lord.
When you're looking for answers, look to the Lord.
When you're looking for someone to tell it straight without a lie,
When you're looking for a friend whose life was given up to die,
Look to the Lord.

When you're looking for someone to hold when you're feeling all alone,
When you're looking for a friend that you call your very own,
There is one who stands beside you, who wants to give to you His all;
Look to the Lord.

OCTOBER '97

Once again, lyrics but no tune. God works in mysterious ways. But if He gives it to you, you better write it down. There is always a reason.

"Give Your Life to Jesus"

Give your hand to Jesus, He will lead the way,
He will watch your every step, guide you all the way.
And as you travel life's ups and downs, you may lose your way;
Give your hand to Jesus, He will lead the way.

Give your heart to Jesus, He will understand,
He will love and comfort you, hold you by the hand.
When life's shadows close on you and questions enter in,
Give your heart to Jesus, He will understand.

> *He's always waiting for you,*
> *He will always be there.*
> *No matter what you do,*
> *I just can't explain,*
> *I know that He answers when you call,*
> *When you call upon His name.*

Give your life to Jesus, He's the only one,
Chosen by His Father, He's God's only Son.

John M. Reichert

He sacrificed to give you life, and victory over death, He's won.
Give your life to Jesus, He's the only one,
Give your life to Jesus, He's the only one.

NOVEMBER '97

There is an old hymn, "I Surrender All," written by Winfield Weeden and Judson van de Venter. I so enjoy this hymn. This is a combination of their song and the one God gave to me.

"Surrender"

"I surrender all. I surrender all. All to thee, my blessed Savior, I surrender all."

> *Have you given your all to Him?*
> *Have you given your all to the Father?*
> *Have you held nothing back, hid something away?*
> *Can you humbly bow your head and say,*

"I surrender all. I surrender all. All to thee, my blessed Savior, I surrender all."

> *Have you emptied your soul to the Lord?*
> *Have you emptied and poured out your heart?*
> *Have you given your burdens, your soul to give rest?*
> *Do you know that He'll not settle for less?*

"I surrender all. I surrender all. All to thee, my blessed Savior, I surrender all."

>Surrender is relinquishing all that we hold dear
>To the One of higher power,
>To the One who holds all things in His hands.
>
>Have you given to Him first place?
>Have you placed Him above all the others?
>Have you made Him your Lord, made Him your King?
>Do you lift your hands to God and sing?

"I surrender all. I surrender all. All to thee, my blessed Savior, I surrender all.
All to thee, my blessed Savior, I surrender all."

Matthew 13:43 (KJV) says, "Then shall the righteous shine forth as the sun in the Kingdom of their Father…" This is one of Steve's favorites because it's blue grassy, and he uses his upright bass! I've got to say I like it too!!!

"Shine Like the Sun"

No shadow can exist in the brightness of His glory,
No darkness will persist in the brightness of His throne.
No longer will there be, crying, tears, and sadness
When we come to see that kingdom, that kingdom as our home.

>*I want to shine like the sun*
>*In the kingdom of the Father.*
>*I want to drive out every shadow,*

> make a brighter light.
> I want to shine like the sun
> In the kingdom of the Father,
> Where the day is ever-lasting,
> and there never comes a night.

No longer will the stars shine out in the heavens,
It will not be dark enough to let their twinkle through.
No longer will the moon shine out in the darkness;
There will be no light that shines as bright as You.

> I want to shine like the sun
> In the kingdom of the Father.
> I want to drive out every shadow,
> make a brighter light.
> I want to shine like the sun
> In the kingdom of the Father,
> Where the day is ever-lasting,
> and there never comes a night.

Then all the saints, in their robes of white,
Will gather at God's throne and reflect His royal light.

> I want to shine like the sun
> In the kingdom of the Father.
> I want to drive out every shadow,
> make a brighter light.
> I want to shine like the sun
> In the kingdom of the Father,
> Where the day is ever-lasting,
> and there never comes a night.

John M. Reichert

God gave me another blues song. I wish I could play lead guitar; they seem like they have so much fun, especially on blues tunes.

"Everlasting Love"

Just the other day I was feeling sorry for myself,
Took down all my woe is me, took it right down off the shelf.
But before I could partake, He said, "What are you thinking of?
What you need is a big O' dose of My everlasting love."

I was feeling way down, feeling way down and low,
I didn't know who to turn to, didn't know which way to go.
When He taps me on the shoulder and He says, "Now look here, son.
Here's another overflowing cup of My everlasting love."

> *He gives me everlasting, everlasting love*
> *Coming down like rain, coming down from above.*
> *Like a shower of blessing, like a rainbow up above,*
> *He covers me all over with His everlasting love.*

(Blues instrumental.)

He takes away my burden, He takes away my cares,
It doesn't matter where I am; He always meets me there.
He floats His blessings 'round me on the prayer wing of a dove,
He pours it all upon me, His everlasting love.

> *He gives me everlasting, everlasting love*
> *Coming down like rain, coming down from above.*

Like a shower of blessing, Like a rainbow up above,
He covers me all over with His everlasting love.

JANUARY '98

This song was a little different for me. It was played with a drop D tuning and had chords like E11/D, Em7, and G6. All things considered, it started out 1998 nicely. Read Psalm 13 (KJV) and Revelation 6:10 (KJV): These are the "How Long" verses.

"How Long"

How long will it be? How long until we see
All the love that He gives us, that He gives to you and me?

How long until we feel His touch until we feel His grace?
How long until we stand before Him and face Him, face to face?

How long will it take before we realize
What love He displayed, what love in sacrifice.

How long until the heavens part before His coming throne?
How long until the kingdom starts, before He brings us home?

instrumental

How long until the heavens part before His coming throne?
How long until the kingdom starts before He brings us home?

How long will the darkness last until the Son breaks through?
How long, Lord, may I ask, until we spend forever with You?

How long will it be, how long until we see
All the love that He gives us, that He gives to you and me?

   How long?
   How long?

Psalm 23 (KJV) says that "He leads me through the valley of the shadow of death, and He leads me beside the still waters…" He cares for me.

It's the same feeling I get at 11,000 feet, sitting on a log with my hands wrapped around a steaming hot cup of coffee on a cold mountain morning! More blues… yes!

"Oh, How He Loves Me"

Oh, how He loves me, oh, how He cares!
He wraps His ever-loving arms around me, lets me know, lets me
   know He is there.
He leads me through the valley of shadow, leads me by the water
   still,
He wants me to trust in His guidance and to do His will.

Oh, how He keeps me in the palm of His hands!
He promised He will never forsake me, on the way, to the promised land.
He'll never, never, never leave me, He's with me all the way,
He brings me so much joy to my soul that I just, I just have to
   say…

> *Oh, how He loves me, oh, how He loves me!*
> *Oh, how He keeps me for His own!*
> *Oh, how He loves me, oh, how He loves me!*
> *And I'm waiting, yes, I'm waiting,*
> *for the day He brings me home.*

Oh, how He loves me; He is my friend,
And if all the others just walk away, He'll be there, He'll be there 'till the end.
If I ever really need Him, I just close my eyes and pray.
He's always there to answer my call—yesterday, tomorrow, today.

> *Oh, how He loves me, oh, how He loves me!*
> *Oh, how He keeps me for His own!*
> *Oh, how He loves me, oh, how He loves me!*
> *And I'm waiting, yes, I'm waiting,*
> *for the day He brings me home.*

FEBRUARY '98

As Jesus was choosing His twelve disciples, I picture Him walking by and calling them by name and telling them to come and follow Him. The disciples just dropped whatever they were doing, left home, friends, and family, and followed Jesus. Are you willing to pay the cost today if Jesus calls?

"What Is the Cost?"

What is the cost of following Jesus?
What is the price to pay?
Wherever He leads, are you willing to follow?
What is the cost today?

What is the cost of following Jesus?
What is the price to pay?
Wherever He leads, are you willing to follow?
What is the cost today?

What is the cost today?

> *Abraham was asked to leave his family;*
> *would you do the same?*
> *All his life, his God, walked beside him;*
> *Friend of God became his name.*

John M. Reichert

What is the cost of following Jesus?
What is the price to pay?
Wherever He leads, are you willing to follow?
What is the cost today?

What is the cost of following Jesus?
What is the price to pay?
Wherever He leads, are you willing to follow?
What is the cost today?

What is the cost today?

> *James and John were asked to leave their fishing nets*
> *and follow Him by the sea.*
> *There, upon the sand, the empty boats sit*
> *by the Sea of Galilee.*

What is the cost of following Jesus?
What is the price to pay?
Wherever He leads, are you willing to follow?
What is the cost today?

What is the cost of following Jesus?
What is the price to pay?
Wherever He leads, are you willing to follow?
What is the cost today?

What is the cost today?

> *It is written—you must deny yourself*
> *and take up your cross,*
> *Give your heart, your might, and all your soul—*
> *that's all it cost.*

What is the cost of following Jesus?
What is the price to pay?
Wherever He leads, are you willing to follow?
What is the cost today?

What is the cost of following Jesus?
What is the price to pay?
Wherever He leads, are you willing to follow?
What is the cost today?

What is the cost today?

John M. Reichert

MAY '98

For all the things that happened to Jesus, He is still my Lord. His birth, suffering, mocking, crucifixion, and resurrection; He is still King of Kings, He is Lord.

"Isn't He Lord?"

Isn't He brave? Isn't He strong
To let the Roman guards mock Him all night long?
Isn't He the one they said would rule the world and set His people free?
Isn't He the one they said would come and be their King?

Isn't He pale, lifeless, and gray
Hanging there upon the cross in the middle of the day?
Isn't He the one who bares the nails in His feet and in His hands?
Isn't He the one who came to be God's sacrificed lamb?

> *Isn't He Lord, Isn't He Lord?*
> *Isn't He sitting by the Father, according to His Word?*
> *Isn't He the one who said He'd come back and reign forever more?*
> *Isn't He King, Isn't He King, Isn't He Lord?*

Isn't He there, where He was laid,
But the stone is rolled away from the opening of the grave?

Isn't He the one who said He'd rise again to live eternally?
Isn't He the one who said He'd die for you and me?

> Isn't He Lord, Isn't He Lord?
> Isn't He sitting by the Father, according to His Word?
> Isn't He the one who said He'd come back and reign forever more?
> Isn't He King, Isn't He King, Isn't He Lord?

Isn't He true, true to His Word,
When He said He'd bring a kingdom and rule it on this world?
Isn't He the one who said to watch for Him morning, night, and noon?
Isn't He the one who said that He'd be coming soon?

> Isn't He Lord, Isn't He Lord?
> Isn't He sitting by the Father, according to His Word?
> Isn't He the one who said He'd come back and reign forever more?
>
> Isn't He King, Isn't He King, Isn't He Lord?
> Isn't He King, Isn't He King, Isn't He Lord?

John M. Reichert

JULY '98

Ever been on one of those detours God puts you on to mature you and get you ready for your destiny? I was. I had quit my job because of ethical reasons, was going through a divorce, and my mom was in a rehab center due to a subdural hematoma. DETOUR. I ended up buying my hometown pharmacy with no money down!! The last thing I ever expected to do! Divine intervention!! I felt God calling me to do this, so I was willing to follow. Listen to Him when He speaks to you!

"I Will Follow"

When You call, I hear Your voice,
like the sheep who hears the shepherd.
With my all, I will make my choice,
and follow, follow You.

Where you lead, I will follow.
Where You show me, I will go.
Where You lead, I will follow,
I will follow, follow You.

Where You lead, I will take my steps
like a blind man walking slowly,
In Your keeping, my soul is kept,
so I will follow You.

Where you lead, I will follow.
Where You show me, I will go.
Where You lead, I will follow,
I will follow, follow You.

I will follow where You lead me,
I will go where You show.
I will follow where You lead me,
I will follow, follow You.

Where you lead, I will follow,
Where You show me, I will go.
Where You lead, I will follow,
I will follow, follow You.

John M. Reichert

AUGUST '98

That simple Sunday school tune kept going over and over in my head one day; you know it, *I will make you fishers of men, fishers of men, fishers of men...*

Even the "experts" tried to tell Jesus about fishing, and He told them to cast their nets into deep water. Can you hear them mumbling, "He doesn't know what He's talking about"? When Jesus tells you to do something that doesn't go along with the natural, get ready for something big to happen! Are we fishing in deep water?

"Deep Water"

What is the lure when you're fishing for men?
What is the tackle that you use?
Do you cast far when you try to reel them in
What is the bait that you use?

> *Cast your nets into deep water;*
> *There the fishes will be more.*
> *Cast your nets into deep water*
> *And pull them to the shore, and pull them to the shore.*

Are you real, or are you artificial
When you witness for the Lord?
Are you humble, or are you something special
When you're cast into the world?

Cast your nets into deep water;
There the fishes will be more.
Cast your nets into deep water
And pull them to the shore, and pull them to the shore.

Don't miss the bobber when it slips below the surface;
How will you know when you've won one for Him?

Cast your nets into deep water;
There the fishes will be more.
Cast your nets into deep water
And pull them to the shore, and pull them to the shore.

"I will make you fishers of men, fishers of men, fishers of men…"

This next song was written for my daughter Erin just before she left for college in Atlanta, GA. The writing of the song was easy compared to singing the song for her. The message still holds true today. At this writing, she is the mother of five of my beautiful grandchildren and working on her teaching degree; Erin is truly an awesome woman. There is none like her!

"In My Heart"

In my heart, you will stay,
Though you move far away.
You must know, though you leave,
Part of you stays with me.

All the years come and go,
And the time quickly flies.

But wherever you go,
You must now realize…

> *Whether far, whether near,*
> *You will always be here.*
> *In my heart, every day,*
> *In my heart, you will stay.*

There are times that are sad,
There are times that we smile,
And the love that we have
Will traverse every mile.

> *Whether far, whether near,*
> *You will always be here.*
> *In my heart, every day,*
> *In my heart, you will stay.*

> *Whether far, whether near,*
> *You will always be here.*
> *In my heart, you will stay,*
> *Though you move far away.*

> *You must know, though you leave,*
> *Part of you stays with me.*

For I have often heard said,
"Out of sight, out of head."
But in my heart, every day,
In my heart, you will stay.

> *In my heart, every day,*
> *In my heart, you will stay.*

MARCH '99

My mom passed away in January 1999; she was one week short of being eighty-two years old. God has a designated time for us to go, some sooner and some later. I kept praying and telling Mom that she could beat this and that she would get better. A nurse told me that maybe she was hanging on, waiting to know if I'd be alright. Maybe she needed to hear me say so and that it was okay to go be with Jesus. I had been sitting by her bedside, and I whispered in her ear that I was going to be fine, "go be with Jesus, Mom." My work beeper alarmed. I called my brother Joel to see if he could come sit with Mom. I hadn't been gone thirty minutes when Joel called to tell me Mom had passed. Sometimes we need to let them go be glorious! I didn't feel much like writing during that time, but God eventually worked me through this.

This was one of those "no music" songs, in other words, just lyrics. Somebody, please write a melody for "Answer to Your Song."

"Answer to Your Song"

Who do you talk to when you're feeling down and blue?
Who do you talk to when you're feeling down and blue?
Who do you lean on when you don't know what to do?

Who do you turn to when your heart is in decline?
Who do you turn to when your heart is in decline?
Who do you look for when a friend you cannot find?

> *I know you think about it all the time,*
> *I don't know if it's right or wrong.*
> *With a little patience, I know you will find*
> *The answer to your song.*

Don't you know who loves you when you think nobody cares?
Don't you know who loves you when you think nobody cares?
Don't you think it's funny Jesus knows your every prayer?

> *I know you think about it all the time,*
> *I don't know if it's right or wrong.*
> *With a little patience, I know you will find*
> *The answer to your song.*

Don't you know who loves you when you think nobody cares?
Don't you know who loves you when you think nobody cares?
Don't you think it's funny Jesus knows your every prayer?
Don't you think it's funny Jesus knows your every prayer?

APRIL '99

I believe that God holds all things in His hands. Satan is trying to create chaos in this world and in heavenly places, but all things must pass through God's hands first. Satan is still God's creation.

I can think of no safer place to be than in God's hand.

"Forever"

Wrapped inside Your arms, forever,
You are the love of my life.
Keep me safe from harm, forever,
You are the Lord of my life.

> *You are the Lord, forever the Lord,*
> *You are the Lord of my life.*

Wrapped inside your arms forever,
You are the Lord of my life.
Standing in Your palm, forever,
You hold my life in Your hand.
There is always calm, forever,
Safe in the palm of Your hand.

> *Safe in Your palm, forever in calm,*
> *Safe in the palm of Your hand.*

Standing in Your palm, forever,
You hold my life in Your hand.
Wrapped inside Your arms forever,
You are the love of my heart.
Keep me safe and warm, forever,
You are the Lord of my heart.

> *You are the Lord, forever the Lord,*
> *You are the Lord of my heart.*

Wrapped inside Your arms, forever,
You are the Lord of my heart.
You are the Lord, forever the Lord,
You are the Lord of my heart.

Psalm 148 (KJV) speaks of all creation praising the Lord. In verse 5, it states, "Let them praise the name of the Lord: for He commanded, and they were created." Another April song this year.

"Praise the Name of the Lord"

Old men and children, young men and maidens,
Let them praise the name of the Lord.
Kings of the earth and rulers of nations,
Let them praise the name of the Lord.

> *Let them rejoice with the song of the voice*
> *And praise the name of the Lord.*
> *Let them lift high their anthem of choice*

And praise the name of the Lord.

Lightning and wind, the hail and the snow,
Let them praise the name of the Lord.
The stars up above and the mountains below,
Let them praise the name of the Lord.

Let them cry out, let their noise shout on high,
And praise the name of the Lord.
Lifting their praise on the wings of the sky
And praise the name of the Lord.

> *From the lips of the infants and children,*
> *You ordained praise.*
> *Even the blades of the grass*
> *lift up their praise to Your Name.*

Praise Him, you host of heavenly angels,
Praise the name of the Lord.
Praise Him the most and the least of the ages,
Praise the name of the Lord.

> *Now to rejoice, rejoice in salvation,*
> *Praise the name of the Lord.*
> *Give thanks to the Father, the Lord of creation,*
> *Praise the name of the Lord.*

> *Let us praise the name of the Lord*
> *Let us praise the name of the Lord.*

John M. Reichert

The third song that God gave me in April 1999 ended up being one of the band's favorites. Although simple in structure, it holds great meaning. God is a God of Love, and His Love is unmeasurable and endless.

"Great Is Your Love"

I pray to You, Lord, in the time of Your favor,
For great is Your love.
Rescue me now, O Lord and my Savior,
For great is Your love.

> *Do not hide Your face from me,*
> *Come now, Lord, and rescue me.*
> *Come and pour Your love on me.*

I pray to You, Lord, in the time of Your mercy,
For great is Your love.
Come to me now, in the time of my hurting,
For great is Your love.

> *Your mercy, O Lord, reaches the sky,*
> *You deliver the weak when upward they cry.*
> *Come use Your love to dry my eyes.*

> *Great is the Lord,*
> *Great is Your love.*
> *Great is the Lord,*
> *Great is Your love.*

I sing to You, Lord, in the time of Your pleasure,
For great is Your love.
Come fill me now with the fullness of measure,
For great is Your love.

Come and turn Your smile on me.
Come now, Lord, renew me,
Lift me to eternity.

Great is Your love
Great is Your love
Great is Your love.

John M. Reichert

JULY '99

Hebrews 2: 6–7 (KJV) says, "…what is man that Thou art mindful of him? or the son of man, that Thou visits him? Thou madest him a little lower than the angels; thou crownedst him with glory and honor, and didst set him over the works of thy hands."

I have no idea why God is mindful of me, except that He loves me.

"Redeemed"

How can You love me, You never even met me,
And give Your life to die for me?
How can You take my sins and wear them on Your shoulders
And help the lost to be redeemed?

You are the Son of God, the Chosen, the Messiah,
Your Father's will, You did obey.
And by Your dying, You opened up the kingdom
And drove the darkness all away.

> *I know I'm placed a little lower than the angels*
> *Still, this is held with some esteem.*
> *I know some nails are always bent throughout the ages,*
> *But You're the one who can redeem.*

I know I'm placed a little lower than the angels
Still, this is held with some esteem.
I know some nails are always bent throughout the ages,
But You're the one who can redeem.

How can You love me, You never even met me
And give Your life to die for me.
And by Your dying, You opened up the kingdom
And helped me, lost, to be redeemed.

John M. Reichert

OCTOBER '99

Philippians 4:19 (KJV) says, "But my God shall supply all you need according to his riches in glory by Christ Jesus." And take the time to read Matthew 6: 9–34. Even King Solomon was not adorned as royally as the lilies of the field. God is my source. He has never ever not met a need that I have had. He constantly provides for me, and I worship Him for it.

"Answer to My Need"

When I look into the sky and I see the birds that fly,
I know for sure there is a God above.
I know He cares for me by the way He dresses these,
I know for sure He is a God of love.

When I get up in the morning and I'm looking to the East,
The sun is on the rise, and day has come.
He brings the manna from the sky,
He wets my lips when they are dry,
The Lord is the provider, He is one.

> He is the answer, He is the answer to my needs;
> He is the answer, He is the answer to my needs.

When I lie awake at night and the stars are shining bright,
I know my God holds all within His hands.

My needs have all been heard way before I speak a word,
I know my God is always close at hand.

He is the answer, He is the answer to my needs

God helped me buy my hometown pharmacy with no money down. There was no way possible that I could have made this deal happen. I was working on financing through a pharmaceutical wholesaler and had been dealing with a certain person. We had been keeping in close contact, and he was going on vacation, said he'd have an answer on financing for me when he returned. I didn't hear, and I didn't hear, so I called. I was told that he passed away while on vacation, and there was no paperwork record of our dealings. This is when the hometown bank came to the rescue and financed the pharmacy. God is good!!! All the time!!! Everything I am or have belongs to God!

"Every Word, Every Line"

Lord, I lift my praise to You when I sing Your songs for You,
All I have is Yours, not mine—every word and every line.

> *I sing my praise to Thee,*
> *Almighty God and King.*
> *All I have, to You, I gladly bring.*

Lord, let every eye that sees come to believe in Thee,
Let them understand Your tears, let every ear that hears.

> *Let them see Your suffering,*
> *Hear the shouts of Praise His Name,*

Humbly give their all before the King.

I come before the King,
On my knees, I gladly lean,
And at His feet, I lay my everything.

Lord, I lift my praise to You when I sing these songs for You,
All I have is Yours, not mine— Every word and every line.

NOVEMBER '99

There is an old hymn, "Trust and Obey," authored by John H Sammis in 1887. "Trust and obey, for there's no other way to be happy in Jesus but to trust and obey." With every step, I trust Jesus.

"My Jesus"

My Jesus, I love You.
My Jesus, I need You.

> *Every hour of every day,*
> *You walk beside me along the way.*

My Jesus, I love You.
My Jesus, I need You.

> *With every step, You take my hand,*
> *You show the way, You are my friend.*

My Jesus, I love You.
My Jesus, I need You.

> *As time moves on, and changes are,*
> *You are as constant as every star, my Jesus.*
>
> *Like the rising of the moon, like the setting of the sun,*
> *Like a timelessness forgotten, Your love goes on and on.*

John M. Reichert

My Jesus, I love You.
My Jesus, I need You.

> *You're all I need, You're everything,*
> *You are my Lord, You are my King.*

My Jesus, I love You.
My Jesus, I need You.
My Jesus, I love You.
My Jesus, I need You.

JANUARY '00

Now a promise made is a debt unpaid, and the trail has its own stern code. In the days to come, though my lips were dumb, in my heart, how I cursed that load.

— Robert Service
The Cremation of Sam McGee

I had purchased my hometown pharmacy. I had one full-time employee and three part-time employees. We were open 9–6 Monday through Friday, 8–12 on Saturdays, and closed on Sunday.

When I started writing songs for God, I vowed to Him that I would write one song a month for His glory. The promise made! Up to this point, there had passed 156 months, and God had given me 153 songs to write down. If you have been counting, there are 150 so far. That's because three songs were lyrical rewrites of secular songs and, for copyright reasons, are not included here. I was pretty much right on schedule.

Being the owner of a small business, I found out that not only was I the owner and pharmacist, I was also the janitor, stock boy, ordering clerk, and accountant. I was so overwhelmed, and I did something I have regretted ever since. I asked God to release me of my pledge of one song a month, and He did. The debt unpaid! Each year the songs got fewer, and there were some years no songs were given to me. Every now and then, God gives me a song, and I do my best to get it on paper.

I should have trusted God more that He would help me run the business and keep my pledge. I can hear Jesus saying, "Oh ye of little faith!" It has left me with an empty feeling inside. That feeling when you let someone down that's counting on you. "…though my lips were dumb, in my heart, how I cursed that load."

So, when God told me to write all my songs down in this book, I jumped on it. I did not want to disappoint my Jesus again! So let us keep going.

"Take My Friend"

You have walked a long and winding road;
have you always walked this road alone?
You say the journey sometimes seems quite tough,
and the road is never smooth enough.

> *What are friends for but to give a helping hand*
> *And raise the road to meet your feet?*
> *They hold your door; they level out the land*
> *And help you know what to believe.*

I've a friend who walks the road with me,
helps me judge my every mystery.
I can call my Friend at any time;
there's no better Friend to find.

> *My Friend is Jesus; He's with me every day,*
> *A true companion on my way.*

My Friend is Jesus; make it safe to say
He is the light that shows the way.

Won't you take my Friend along with you?
He will guide in all you say and do.
Won't you take my Friend to be yours too?
Won't you take my Friend along with you?

My Friend is Jesus; He's with me every day,
A true companion on my way.
My Friend is Jesus; make it safe to say
He is the light that shows the way.

Won't you take my Friend to be yours too?
Won't you take my Friend along with you?

John M. Reichert

APRIL '00

The best teacher I ever had was Mr. Ron Smith. He taught all the math classes at Triton High School. It wasn't the subject, but it was the way he taught. Mr. Smith would have you go to the front of the class, at the chalkboard, and he would have you work out the problems. Sometimes he'd have you race with another student. He would have you explain your work, which on more than one occasion would reveal your mistake. It would be at this point that Mr. Smith would slap his head and say, "Mr. Reichert, what were you thinking?" In the senior yearbook, I placed Mr. Smith along with my dad as the two people I admired the most.

"What Was I Thinking"

Sometimes we feel we can just go on and do it our own way,
We tell the Lord and convince ourselves we'll do it another day.
Sometimes I think we should slap ourselves upside the head and
*   say, "What was I thinking?"*

We never realize how many others we affect when we don't obey,
While we sleep away, all those souls that we neglect get tossed in
*   the fray.*
Sometimes I think we should slap ourselves upside the head…and
*   say, "What was I thinking?"*

> *You can run, you can run, far away, you can run,*
> *But the Lord will find you and have some fun.*
> *You can run, you can run, O you can hide,*
> *But in the end, the Lord will decide.*

Three days I spent in the belly of a fish, wishing that fish would learn how to spit.
Three days and now I'm up on the shore, learned my lesson well, going to serve my Lord.
Why does it always take so long to come clean?
You know what I mean.

> *You can run, you can run, far away, you can run,*
> *But the Lord will find you and have some fun.*
> *You can run, you can run, O you can hide,*
> *But in the end, the Lord will decide.*

Sometimes we feel we can just go on and do it our own way,
We tell the Lord and convince ourselves we'll do it another day.
Sometimes I think we should slap ourselves upside the head and say, "What was I thinking?"

"What was I thinking? What was I thinking, Lord?"

John M. Reichert

MAY '00

Walking with God is the best way. There are many people in the Bible who are mentioned to have walked with God. Abraham, Enoch, and others. I'm sure walking with God makes Him smile. May I always walk with God.

"When You Walk With God"

When you walk with God, it's a mighty fine walk,
When you walk with God, it's a mighty fine talk.
When you walk with God to the very end,
When you walk with God, He's a very long friend.

> *He hears all your whispers, and He hears all your prayers,*
> *He hears all your whispers because He's always there.*

When you walk with God, it's a mighty fine walk,
When you walk with God, it's a mighty fine talk.

When you walk with God up and down the road,
When you walk with God, He will carry your load.
When you walk with God, He will be your friend.
When you walk with God, He will hold your hand.

> *He will not forsake you, He will never leave.*
> *He is all you ever wanted; He is all you'll ever need.*

When you walk with God up and down the road,
When you walk with God, He will carry your load.

When you walk with God, do you know what it takes?
When you walk with God and you make a mistake,
Do you beg for forgiveness? Do you beg for your soul?
Do you beg to your Lord that He make you whole?

> *When you ask for forgiveness, He will hear your plea;*
> *When you ask for forgiveness, He will wipe it clean.*

When you walk with God, do you know what it takes?
When you walk with God and you make a mistake.

When you walk with God, it's a mighty fine walk,
When you walk with God, it's a mighty fine talk.
When you walk with God to the very end,
When you walk with God, He's a very long friend.

> *He hears all your whispers, and He hears all your prayers,*
> *He hears all your whispers because He's always there.*

When you walk with God, it's a mighty fine walk,
When you walk with God, it's a mighty fine talk.

John M. Reichert

JULY '00

I am a sinner saved by grace. Not by my works so that I will never brag about it. It takes the Lord to change you, or you will keep making the same mistakes and living your life the same all over again.

"Lord Change Me"

I have walked, and I have talked.
When I've talked the talk, I've failed to walk the walk.
I have sinned, I've sinned them all.
When I've tried to stand up tall, I end up small.

> *So, Lord, change me, O, Lord, change me.*
> *It's the only way that I could ever win.*
> *O, Lord, change me, O, Lord, change me.*
> *If You don't, I'll do them all, all over again.*

I have looked, and I have seen,
But my learning curve is tilted so extreme.
I have failed to do Your will,
But You find it in Your heart to love me still.

> *So, Lord, change me, O, Lord, change me.*
> *It's the only way that I could ever win.*
> *O, Lord, change me, O, Lord, change me.*
> *If You don't, I'll do them all, all over again.*

I have breathed borrowed air.
Lord, You see my heart and soul—they need repair.
Lord, You see the disarray.
Lord, let me live and breathe just one more day.

> *So, Lord, change me, O, Lord, change me.*
> *It's the only way that I could ever win.*
> *O, Lord, change me, O, Lord, change me.*
> *If You don't, I'll do them all, all over again.*

> *You have the might, oh Lord, You have the power,*
> *But I'll need You by my side, every minute, every hour.*

> *So, Lord, change me, O, Lord, change me.*
> *It's the only way that I could ever win.*
> *O, Lord, change me, O, Lord, change me.*
> *If You don't, I'll do them all, all over again.*

John M. Reichert

SEPTEMBER '00

My son, Zachary, was off to college. Although it was within driving distance, those of you who have kids going off to college know that they really never come back. Zach and I are very close, and we spend a good deal of time together. We backpack and fish when we can and spend a weekend together now and then. But at that particular time, it was painful.

"Can't Stand the Pain"

Don't like another cold front moving in, don't like the thunder, lightning, don't like the wind,
Don't like bad weather, when it's all around, don't like the rain, when it's pouring down.

Life without you is lonely and cold; it sits in my heart just like a cold hard stone.
Sometimes it feels just like I can't go on; thinking about you is my daily song.

> *Can't stand the pain, can't stand the pain,*
> *Living every day inside these prison gates.*
> *There's a void down deep inside me that I just can't explain,*
> *Oh, Oh.*

Pray for me now as I pray for you that God will show His grace and see us through,
Look to the future, dare not hold to the past—His hand to sustain us and His mercy to last.

> *Can't stand the pain, can't stand the pain,*
> *Living every day inside these prison gates.*
> *There's a void down deep inside me that I just can't explain,*
> *Oh, Oh.*

Waiting for the day when Christ comes again, joining all His people to worship Him,
There in the valley, we will stand side by side, joy and singing, not a tear in the eye.

> *Can't stand the pain, can't stand the pain,*
> *The bars have all been broken, no more prison gates.*
> *It will all be gone forever when God wipes it away.*

At this writing, Zachary is forty, and a spot of cancer was found on his colon. His stomach had been bothering him, so the doctor scheduled a colonoscopy and endoscopy. During the procedure, they found a small spot of cancer and removed it. Many prayer warriors came to the battlefront and bound Satan from Zach's body. The post report is that they got it all, and there is nothing to worry about. A blessing in that his stomach acted up, leading to a colonoscopy to reveal the cancer. God certainly works in mysterious ways. We are giving praise and honor for total healing today!!!

JANUARY '01

My friend Steve invited me to attend The Country Church with him and participate on the worship, music team. It got me thinking that of all the songs that God has given me to scribe down, none have been a worship chorus per se. In January 2001, God did give me one, but it has never been performed in a church, only as worship in my heart.

"Pray to the Lord"

Pray without ceasing, asking the Lord,
As He instructed us in His Word.
Look to His strength, the giver of all,
Seek with the Spirit, pray to the Lord.

Pray without ceasing, asking the Lord,
As He instructed us in His Word.
Look to His strength, the giver of all,
Seek with the Spirit, pray to the Lord.

> *Ask, and it shall be given.*
> *Seek, and it shall be found.*
> *Knock on the door—*
>   *it will be opened to you.*

Pray without ceasing, asking the Lord,
As He instructed us in His Word.

Look to His strength, the giver of all,
Seek with the Spirit, pray to the Lord.

Seek with the Spirit, pray to the Lord.

SEPTEMBER '01

It was nine months later that God gave me the next song. Remember that I asked to be released from my promise to write one every month. God remembers! In total honor of Him, He gave me Yahweh. In the original Hebrew, there were no vowels. It was just YHWH, which is not pronounceable. It is the name of God!!!

"Yahweh"

Like the sun, like the moon,
I will lift my praise to You.
Like the wind that blows,
Like the clouds that roll.
I will lift my song and let You know.

> *Honor and Glory are for You, O Lord;*
> *All creation gives its praise.*
> *Your name echoes through the galaxy—*
> *Yahweh, Yahweh, Yahweh.*

Like the trees that rise,
Like the stars at night,
There's no equal to Your place.
In the storms that rage,
In my day to day,
I will bow myself and lift Your name.

Honor and Glory are for You, O Lord;
All creation gives its praise.
Your name echoes through the galaxy—
Yahweh, Yahweh, Yahweh.

The Lord our God, The Lord is one.
The Lord our God, The Lord is one.
The Lord our God, The Lord our God,
The Lord our God is one.

On the eagle's wing,
I will rise and sing,
I will worship as the praises ring.
Like the mountain high,
Rising in the sky,
I will give my praise to You, my King.

Honor and Glory are for You, O Lord;
All creation gives its praise.
Your name echoes through the galaxy—
Yahweh, Yahweh, Yahweh.

John M. Reichert

DECEMBER '01

John 15:4 (KJV) says, "Abide in me, and I in you. As the branch cannot bear fruit of itself, except it abide in the vine; no more can ye, except ye abide in me. vs5: I am the vine, ye are the branches…"

"Abide In Me, Lord"

So that my joy may be complete, O, Lord abide in me,
Keep me fruitful, keep me on my knees in prayer.
O, Lord, You know I need You there.

So that my faith goes on and on, so that my trust grows ever strong,
Keep me loving, keep me walking hand in hand.
Abide in me, Lord, I understand.

> *O, Lord, You are the vine.*
> *I'm just a branch, O, Lord, but I'm Thine.*
> *Keep me with You, night and day.*
> *I need to know, O, Lord, You are with me all the way.*

> *O, Lord, You are the vine.*
> *I'm just a branch, O, Lord, but I'm Thine.*
> *Keep me with You, night and day.*
> *I need to know, O, Lord, You are with me all the way.*

So that my soul may rest in peace, abide in me, Lord, eternally.
Give me comfort, fill me with the Word, Abide in me, Lord, forever more.

Give me comfort, fill me with Your Word,
Abide in me, Lord, forever more.

MARCH '02

I look forward to the day Jesus brings us into His kingdom!! Don't get me wrong, I love this life on earth, in history, but the kingdom of God will be the ultimate place to be. I hope you will be there too! Confess your sins and ask Jesus to save you. Matthew 24:35–36 (KJV) says, "Heaven and earth shall pass away, but my word shall not pass away. But of that day and hour knoweth no man, no, not the angels of heaven, but my Father only."

"Maybe Today"

Maybe today will be the day,
maybe today we'll hear Him say,
"Come and enter, all my faithful servants."

Maybe today we'll win the prize,
maybe we'll look into His eyes,
Maybe today will be the day, maybe today…

Got a list of things to do, don't know where to start,
Got to pray for me and you and all things heavy on my heart.
No one knows what today may bring; at least, that's what they say.
Maybe today will be the day, maybe today…

> *Maybe today will be the day,*
> *maybe today we'll hear Him say,*
> *"Come and enter, all my faithful servants."*
>
> *Maybe today we'll win the prize,*
> *maybe we'll look into His eyes,*
> *Maybe today will be the day, maybe today…*

Help a brother, help a friend, do your Christian best,
There's no telling what time of day we'll stand to take the test.
Persevere for character, build a faith that's strong,
Maybe today we'll hear that song (when the roll), maybe today…

> *Maybe today will be the day,*
> *maybe today we'll hear Him say,*
> *"Come and enter, all my faithful servants."*
>
> *Maybe today we'll win the prize,*
> *maybe we'll look into His eyes,*
> *Maybe today will be the day, maybe today…*

My day is done, my work is through, I've tried to keep the pace,
I haven't always kept the lead while running a good race.
Stay the course, keep true the cause, and if the sun should rise again,
Maybe today He'll call my name, maybe today…

> *Maybe today will be the day,*
> *maybe today we'll hear Him say,*
> *"Come and enter, all my faithful servants."*
>
> *Maybe today we'll win the prize,*
> *maybe we'll look into His eyes,*
> *Maybe today will be the day, maybe today.*

John M. Reichert

Always watch for the clouds to part and the sky to roll away,

>*Maybe today will be the day, maybe today…*

>*Maybe today will be the day,*
>*maybe today we'll hear Him say,*
>*"Come and enter, all my faithful servants."*

>*Maybe today we'll win the prize,*
>*maybe we'll look into His eyes,*
>*Maybe today will be the day, maybe today.*

APRIL '02

Hebrews 12:22 (KJV) says, "But ye are come unto mount Zion, and unto the city of the living God, the heavenly Jerusalem, and to an innumerable company of angels…"

And Revelations 14:1 (KJV) also speaks of standing on Mt. Zion to worship the Lord. A blues tune.

"Stand On the Mountain"

Come on along, along with me,
Across the river and across the sea.
Come on and worship the Son;
We're going to stand on the mountainside and worship the One.

Bring your brother, your sister with you,
Bring your neighbor and your friend and your enemies too.
Come on and worship the Son;
We're going to stand on the mountainside and worship the One.

Yes, you and me—
We'll stand hand in hand together, you'll see.
Come on and worship the Son;
We're going to stand on the mountainside and worship the One.

Across the valley and through the plains,
You must make it there, O, you must find THE WAY.
Come on and worship the Son;

John M. Reichert

We're going to stand on the mountain Zion and worship the One.

> *Sing Hallelujah, Sing praise His name,*
> *Sing glory and honor, forever, amen.*

Come on and worship the Son;
We're going to stand on the mountainside and worship the One.

You hear the trumpet, now don't be late,
You don't want to find yourself standing outside the gate.
Come one and worship the Son,
We're going to stand on the mountainside and worship the One.

We're going to stand on the mountain Zion and worship the One.

MAY '02

God gave me a neat little song to scribe down in May 2002. Nothing can make you as white as snow but the blood of Jesus.

"Nothing but the Blood"

Nothing, O, O, nothing, O, O, nothing but the blood of Jesus.
Nothing, O, O, nothing, O, O, nothing but the blood of Jesus.
Nothing, O, O, nothing, O, O, nothing but the blood of Jesus.
Nothing, O, O, nothing, O, O, nothing but the blood of Jesus.

> *He's decided to move out west.*
> *He's decided, this time, to do his best.*
> *He is obviously running, running so fast,*
> *He is running from something in his past.*

Nothing, O, O, nothing, O, O, nothing but the blood of Jesus.
Nothing, O, O, nothing, O, O, nothing but the blood of Jesus.
Nothing, O, O, nothing, O, O, nothing but the blood of Jesus.
Nothing, O, O, nothing, O, O, nothing but the blood of Jesus.

> *She was standing there scrubbing a stain from her clothes,*
> *Scrubbing a stain that God only knows.*
> *She was standing at the altar, scrubbing her heart;*
> *She was working on a brand-new start.*

Nothing, O, O, nothing, O, O, nothing but the blood of Jesus.
Nothing, O, O, nothing, O, O, nothing but the blood of Jesus.
Nothing, O, O, nothing, O, O, nothing but the blood of Jesus.
Nothing, O, O, nothing, O, O, nothing but the blood of Jesus.

Nothing, O, O, nothing, O, O, nothing but the blood of Jesus
Can wash you as white as snow.
Nothing, O, O, nothing, O, O, nothing but the blood of Jesus
Can cleanse you and make you whole.
Nothing, O, O, nothing, O, O, nothing but the blood of Jesus
Can take away your sins.
Nothing, O, O, nothing, O, O, nothing but the blood of Jesus
Can make you live again.

Nothing, O, O, nothing, O, O, nothing but the blood of Jesus.
Nothing, O, O, nothing, O, O, nothing but the blood of Jesus.
Nothing, O, O, nothing, O, O, nothing but the blood of Jesus.
Nothing, O, O, nothing, O, O, nothing but the blood of Jesus.

But the blood of Jesus, but the blood of Jesus,
But the blood of Jesus.

OCTOBER '02

I'm sorry, folks, but I'm getting older!!! Right rotator cuff repair, four knee surgeries, two artificial knees, two broken ankles, broken wrist, and a broken elbow. My joints ache. Especially in the morning and when it's cold outside!! I'd like to say it's the miles and not the years, but I think it's a combination of both. My soul, however, still sings a song.

"My Soul Is Young"

My hair's turned grey, my knees ache with pain,
All of my joints are stiff in the morning.

I'm out of breath when I walk up too many steps,
Sometimes my back gives out without warning, but

> *My soul is young, my soul is young.*
> *When it's held by the One, when it's held by the Son,*
> *My soul is young.*

I don't go fast like I did in the past;
The miles have been long, and the way has been narrow.

My bones grow old as the weather turns oh-so cold,
But deep in my heart sings the song of a sparrow.

> *My soul is young, my soul is young.*
> *When it's held by the One, when it's held by the Son,*
> *My soul is young.*

It does not matter what age you see;
All can still serve Him if they will believe.

I won't give up, I won't give in,
With all my heart and strength, I will serve Him.

> *My soul is young, my soul is young.*
> *When it's held by the One, when it's held by the Son,*
> *My soul is young.*

MARCH '03

When I owned my hometown pharmacy, I was working one day, and a man, who went by Ox, came into the store, walked right behind the prescription counter, grabbed me by the hand, held it to the sky, and said, "God told me to come and pray for you!" I know some think that is weird, but I enjoy and need a pray warrior to take my name before God's throne. It is such a great thing to have someone intercede for you in prayer. Ox passed away, and I was wondering who would be my warrior.

"Who's Gonna Pray for Me Now?"

I had a mother; her thing was prayer.
She read her Bible from a rocking chair.
She took my name before the throne;
She said it's good to know you're never alone.

> *Who's gonna be my warrior?*
> *Who's gonna pray for me now?*
> *Who's gonna be my warrior?*
> *Who's gonna pray for me now?*

I had a pastor; he was my friend.
He said he'd pray for me until the very end.
He died one summer; there was no clue.
I wonder who will fill his praying shoes.

John M. Reichert

> *Who's gonna be my warrior?*
> *Who's gonna pray for me now?*
> *Who's gonna be my warrior?*
> *Who's gonna pray for me now?*

My brother Ox; he prayed for me.
He spent his lifetime down on his knees.
He faced the devil both day and night;
He quoted scriptures in the heat of the fight.

> *Who's gonna be my warrior?*
> *Who's gonna pray for me now?*
> *Who's gonna be my warrior?*
> *Who's gonna pray for me now?*

MAY '03

This one is right out of Ecclesiastes.

"Chasing After the Wind"

The sun rises in the east, the sun sets in the west,
The sun hurries back around to rise again and then go down.
A time appointed to be born, a time appointed once to die;
There is a time for peace and war; there is a time to laugh and cry.

> *Here we go again, chasing after the wind;*
> *It runs here, it runs there.*
> *You try to catch it, and your hands are full*
> *Of nothing but air*
> *Chasing after the wind.*

There is a time to build things up; there is a time to tear it down.
There is a time for peace and love and to be laid down in the ground.

> *Here we go again, chasing after the wind;*
> *It runs here, it runs there.*
> *You try to catch it, and your hands are full*
> *Of nothing but air*
> *Chasing after the wind.*

John M. Reichert

A man labors in the heat, a man labors in the cold;
A boy labors when he's young, a man labors when he's old.
A man should give the Lord his first; a man should give the Lord his best;
A foolish chasing of the wind, he rises up and works again.

> *Here we go again, chasing after the wind;*
> *It runs here, it runs there.*
> *You try to catch it, and your hands are full*
> *Of nothing but air*
> *Chasing after the wind.*

MARCH '04

John 15:12–13 (KJV) says, "This is my commandment, that ye love one another, as I have loved you. Greater love hath no man than this, that a man lay down his life for his friends"

"If You Were Me"

If you were me, what would you say to help a friend in need?
If you were me and I were you, how would you help this friend believe?

If you were me and time was still, frozen in the truth of love,
Then hope could see and faith could breathe and hearts begin to rise above.

If I were you, I'd share Jesus, no greater love deep in your heart,
The spirit, too, to love and guide us, for it can heal the wounded heart.

If I were you, I'd speak the truth and fill your words with compassion,
And maybe then, this friend would feel the love of Christ's passion.

If you were me and I were you, how would you help a friend believe?
The love of God is one from two. If I were you and you were me.

If I were you, if you were me.

John M. Reichert

NOVEMBER '04

Sometimes when you are going through a tough time, only God knows exactly what you need. Remember when Sarah was told at the age of eighty-five she would have a child? She laughed. And when that baby boy was born, it was named laughter: Isaac! November 2004 brought laughter to me…my grandson, Isaac.

"Laughter Came"

I felt my life fill with sadness, sorrow, and despair,
Dark clouds filled the sky; raindrops filled the air.

I'd forgotten every dark cloud has a lining that will shine,
The joy of God comes shining through, but only in His time.

I've heard it said it's the little things that make life so worthwhile:
A gentle word, a tender touch, an unexpected smile.

> *Then laughter came, and Gabriel sang,*
> *And all of heaven shouted forth with praise.*
> *Because laughter came, and on that day,*
> *A smile appeared upon God's face.*

Sometimes miracles happen, but we just can't believe;
How could this miracle happen? How could it happen to me?

Like Abraham and Sarah thought when they first were told
A baby boy would soon be born, though they thought they were too old.

> *Then laughter came, and Gabriel sang,*
> *And all of heaven shouted forth with praise.*
> *Because laughter came, and on that day,*
> *A smile appeared upon God's face.*

So, when the storms of life cloud and dim your sight,
And the hurt inside is so strong it makes you want to cry,
He, who is within you, is greater than without
The peace and joy that dwells within should make you want to shout.

> *Then laughter came, and Gabriel sang,*
> *And all of heaven shouted forth with praise.*
> *Because laughter came, and on that day,*
> *A smile appeared upon God's face.*
>
> *God smiled the day that laughter came.*

John M. Reichert

MAY '05

Psalm 25:15 (NIV) says, "My eyes are ever on the Lord, for only he will release my feet from the snare." God only gave me one song in 2005, but the meaning is still true today and will be true tomorrow also.

"See Me Through"

Your day is like a thousand years;
My days seem like a lifetime.
For every smile and joy, there have been tears;
Still, I hold to You.

What others mean for bad, You turn to good
For those who love You, Lord.
I'll keep holding to Your steady hand,
Because You see me through.

>*So, I praise You, yes, I praise You.*
>*My God will see me through, He will see me through.*
>*I've read His Word; I claim His promises true.*
>*My God will see me through.*

You have seen me through the darkest night;
Your light still shines on me.
I run the race, O, Lord, I fight the good fight,
I lift my praise to You.

You see me through the anger, You see me through the pain;
You see me through the sunshine, cover me when it rains.
You walk beside me when the road is long;
My God sees me through.

> *So, I praise You, yes, I praise You.*
> *My God will see me through, He will see me through.*
> *I've read His Word; I claim His promises true.*
> *My God will see me through.*

I will never leave you; I will never forsake you
I will always see you through
I will carry your burdens; give you rest when you are weary.
I am God; My love will see you through.

> *So, I praise You, yes, I praise You.*
> *My God will see me through, He will see me through.*
> *I've read His Word; I claim His promises true.*
> *My God will see me through.*

John M. Reichert

JANUARY '06

One song in 2006, and it was a Christmas song. Like all kids, my grandson is always wanting to be first. First at this and first at that. "Come on, grandpa, race me. I'm first." It got me thinking about all the firsts which occurred when the baby Jesus was born.

"The First"

They were the first to know of His coming,
Chosen by God to announce His Son's birth.
They filled the air with trumpets and singing,
Announcing Good News to those of the earth.

> *And the angels sang, "Glory to God in the highest.*
> *Peace on the earth, Hallelujah.*
> *Let every man know Emmanuel has come."*

She was the first blessed among women,
She was the first to dry the child's eyes.
Held in her arms, there in the stable,
The child who made angels fill up the sky.

> *And the angels sang, "Glory to God in the highest.*
> *Peace on the earth, Hallelujah.*
> *Let every man know Emmanuel has come."*

They were the first to travel the distance,
Leaving their flocks to worship the King.
They were the first to follow a new star;
They were the first their treasures to bring.

> *And the angels sang, "Glory to God in the highest.*
> *Peace on the earth, Hallelujah.*
> *Let every man know Emmanuel has come."*

Emmanuel has come.

John M. Reichert

DECEMBER '08

I taught myself to play chords on the piano. It's enough to entertain myself. There were no songs given to me by God in 2007. In 2008, God gave me four instrumentals, two in August and two in September. August instrumentals were "Audrey" and "Ikey's Song." The September instrumentals were "LULU Mountain," a song about one of my most favorite backpacking destinations, and "Butterflies and Angels." God gave me a cowboy song at the end of the year.

"Cut One Out for Me"

Cut one out for me, cut one out for me.
Morgan, quarter, two-eyed Jack:
It really doesn't matter to me.
I need one ready to ride with Jesus
when He rides to victory;
Cut one out for me, cut one out for me.

God needs cowboys up in heaven to handle His Holy herd,
To rope and ride, to bronc and break, and get them ready to serve.
To get them ready to cross over Jordan into the promised land,
God needs cowboys up in heaven to lend a cowboy hand.

Cut one out for me, cut one out for me.
Morgan, quarter, two-eyed Jack:

> *It really doesn't matter to me.*
> *I need one ready to ride with Jesus*
> *when He rides to victory;*
> *Cut one out for me, cut one out for me.*

There'll be time for mending fences; there'll be time for telling tales.
There'll be time for cleaning out the stalls and some barn sitting as well.
There'll be time for talking to Gene and Roy, time for talking to Sarge and Bill—
Yes, God needs cowboys up in heaven, doing the Father's will.

> *Cut one out for me, cut one out for me.*
> *A paint, a bay, a palomino—*
> *the color's not important, you see.*
> *I just need one ready to ride with Jesus*
> *when He rides to victory;*
> *Cut one out for me, cut one out for me.*

When you walk that narrow road inside the pearly gates,
There'll be cowboys waiting for you to hand you your bridle and reins.
If you haven't picked one yet, just smile at the cowboy and say:

> *Cut one out for me, cut one out for me.*
> *Morgan, quarter, two-eyed Jack:*
> *It really doesn't matter to me.*
> *I need one ready to ride with Jesus*
> *when He rides to victory;*
> *Cut one out for me, cut one out for me.*

John M. Reichert

FEBRUARY '09

Love between a man and a woman is a covenant. The covenant is three-way, man, woman, and God. I think the "older" generation believed in this more than today's generation. They would stick it out through thick and thin and make it last. Today is a "throw-away" generation. Just go buy a new one. I believe, if possible, in making it last, until the end.

"Until the End"

Some things nowadays just don't seem to last;
What's called love today is not like love from the past.
Torn apart and broken up, never seems to mend,
Why can't we make it last until the end?

The way our grand folks stuck it out through thick and thin,
They vowed to see it through until the very end.
They held each other close, called each other friend;
When they said "I love you," it meant until the end.

>   *Until the end, until the end,*
>   *Until the end of forever and ever more.*

There's a love that endures, the length of time—
It can be yours, O, it can be mine.
The love of Jesus is strength; it will never bend;
He will wrap you in His loving arms until the end.

> *Until the end, until the end,*
> *Until the end of forever and ever more.*

There's a woman in my life, O, she loves me dear,
She has my love within her heart, she keeps me near.
She holds me close and calls me her best friend;
I will love her with the love of Jesus until the end.

> *Until the end, until the end,*
> *Until the end of forever and ever more.*
> *I will love her with the love of Jesus until the end.*

John M. Reichert

AUGUST '09

God took the children of Israel through the wilderness after they left Egypt. A journey to the promised land, which should take 2–3 weeks, ended up lasting forty years. Why? God wanted the people to put their entire trust and faith in Him as their sole provider. When they were thirsty, God provided water from a rock. When they were hungry, God brought manna from heaven to feed them. Even then, they did not trust Him completely. Put your trust in God; He will never fail. God is the one and only source!

"I Trust You"

I take a look behind me to see where I have been.
I see the long and winding road that brought me where I am.
I know some nights were moonless, some days the sun did burn;
You were always with me through each and every turn.

> *I trust You, Lord, each and every day.*
> *I trust You, Lord, to guide me on my way.*
> *With your grace and love and mercy,*
> *You lead me by the hand.*
> *I trust You, Lord, I trust You.*

I know sometimes I wandered; I know sometimes I strayed.
I know sometimes I lost the path; sometimes I walked away.

But I always hear You whisper, hear You calling out my name;
You draw me close beside You and love me just the same.

> I trust You, Lord, each and every day.
> I trust You, Lord, to guide me on my way.
> With your grace and love and mercy,
> You lead me by the hand.
> I trust You, Lord, I trust You.
>
> There will always be mountains I feel that I must climb.
> There will always be valleys deep and wide.
> There will always be rivers I know that I must cross.
> There will always be times that I feel that I am lost, so...
>
> I trust You, Lord, each and every day.
> I trust You, Lord, to guide me on my way.
> With your grace and love and mercy,
> You lead me by the hand.
> I trust You, Lord, I trust You.

John M. Reichert

NOVEMBER '09

Remember the story of Jesus' triumphal entry into Jerusalem just before His trial and crucifixion? Jesus was coming down from the Mount of Olives, and the multitude was crying out praises to God for Jesus and all the great miracles He had performed. They thought that this was the time when Jesus would become King and overthrow the Roman government. The Pharisees in the crowd bid Jesus to stop the people from crying out, and Jesus said that if the crowd held their peace, the stones would cry out!! All creation WILL praise Him.

"I'm Alive"

I'm alive, I'm alive, I'm alive because of You.
I'm alive, I'm alive, I'm alive because of You.

> *Let the earth ring out Your glory,*
> *Let the trees lift up your praise.*
> *Let the rocks and stones give testimony*
> *To Your Name, Your Holy Name.*

I'm alive, I'm alive, I'm alive because of You.
I'm alive, I'm alive, I'm alive because of You.

> *By Your stripes, I have been healed.*
> *By Your blood, I've been made whole.*
> *By Your birth and death on calvary,*

You saved my soul, You saved my soul.

I'm alive, I'm alive, I'm alive because of You.
I'm alive, I'm alive, I'm alive because of You.

I'm alive, I'm alive, I'm alive because of You.
I'm alive, I'm alive, I'm alive because of You.

Because of You, because of You, because of You, I'm alive.

SEPTEMBER '10

I love being in the mountains. Most all my vacations have been spent backpacking into and up mountains. When I reach an altitude where the trees start thinning out, called tree line, I can see for miles and miles. For some reason, that moment has always made me feel extremely closer to God. I'm not saying you need to climb mountains to be close to God; I'm just saying it's a time when I really feel His presence. And when we reach our destination on a climb, I like to always shake the hand of those with me and say well done!

"Faithful Friend"

High up in the Rockies, where the tree line meets the snow
Where I feel closest to my God, where I long to go
I will climb all day long just to reach the trails end
If you climb the switchbacks with me, I will shake your hand and say,
"Well done, faithful friend, well done, good and faithful friend."

Way down in the valley, where the river runs so deep
You can paddle, O, so slow, or you can run the rapids steep
I will paddle all day long just to reach the journey's end
If you push on with me, I will shake your hand and say,

> *"Well done, faithful friend, well done, good and faithful friend.*
> *Well done, faithful friend, well done, good and faithful friend."*

> *"We have traveled many paths together, heart and soul;*
> *Won't you travel one more, with me, one more road?"*

High up in the heaven where my Savior resides,
Where I will go someday and sit down at His side,
I will serve Him all my life just to hear one day,
I will give Him all my time to hear Him say,

> *"Well done, good and faithful friend, well done, my faithful friend.*
> *Well done, good and faithful friend, well done, good and faithful friend."*

John M. Reichert

OCTOBER '10

I love seeing a beautiful sunrise or sunset here on the farm. And those days that I get to see both remind me that I should be giving Jesus, my Lord, praise and honor all day long.

"Eastern Sky"

There's a light in the eastern sky,
and you know what that signifies:
Another day has dawned to worship Jesus.

> *Give Him praise, give Him honor,*
> *Lift your voice in song.*
> *Give Him praise, give Him honor,*
> *Worship all day long.*
> *Give Him praise, give Him honor,*
> *Lift your voice in song.*
> *Give Him praise, give Him honor,*
> *Worship all day long.*

The sun is high; it's overhead—
the time has come to bow our heads
And thank the Lord for all that He has given us.

> *Give Him praise, give Him honor,*
> *Lift your voice in song.*
> *Give Him praise, give Him honor,*

Worship all day long.
Give Him praise, give Him honor,
Lift your voice in song.
Give Him praise, give Him honor,
Worship all day long.

The western light is fading low;
another day decides to go.
We find our peace and love in His protection.

Give Him praise, give Him honor,
Lift your voice in song.
Give Him praise, give Him honor,
Worship all day long.
There's a light in the eastern sky.

John M. Reichert

JANUARY '21

A little over ten years went by; God gave me no songs to scribe down. I had been thinking about all the evil in the world, and the scripture, 2 Chronicles 7:14, came to mind. The KJV says, "If my people, who are called by my name, shall humble themselves, and pray, and seek my face, and turn from their wicked ways; then I will hear from heaven, and will forgive their sin, and will heal their land." There is no more urgent time than now to do this!!

"Heal the Land"

Lord, I'm down here on my knees.
I offer up my plea.
Lord, heal the land.

Lord, I humbly look for You.
I repent of all I do.
Lord, heal the land.

> *Lord, heal the land, I pray,*
> *Heal the land today.*
> *Lord, hear me,*
> *You've healed it all before.*
> *Hear me knocking at Your door.*
> *Lord, hear me,*
> *Lord, heal the land.*

Lord, heal us from within,
Heal our hearts, take our sin.
Lord, heal the land.

Lord, take away the wrong,
Take it till it's gone.
Lord, heal the land.

> *Lord, heal the land, I pray,*
> *Heal the land today.*
> *Lord, hear me.*
> *You've healed it all before.*
> *Hear me knocking at Your door.*
> *Lord, hear me*
> *Lord, heal the land.*
>
> *Lord, I'm down here on my knees;*
> *Lord, heal the land.*

Mary and Martha were really upset with Jesus. Their brother Lazarus was sick, sick unto death.

The ladies had called for Jesus to come and heal Lazarus, for they knew Jesus could. But Jesus delayed coming. Lazarus died. When Jesus got there, He received a lecture on biology and impatience. Jesus simply said, "Move the stone." The discourse in biology continued, and Jesus' response remained, "Move the stone." It's great to have faith, but Jesus is looking for the action to back up your faith. How many times are you waiting for your miracle when you have yet to move the stone?

John M. Reichert

"Move the Stone"

Lord, why did You wait?
Why did You hesitate?
Where were You, Lord?

Lord, what took You so long,
Your timing's, O, so wrong,
where were You, Lord?

> *Then I heard the words You said,*
> *It did not settle in my head, move the stone.*

Lord, I thought You were a friend,
said You'd love us till the end.
Where were You, Lord?

Lord, we always look to You;
You do the things You say You'll do.
Where were You, Lord?

> *Still, I heard the words You said,*
> *It did not settle in my head, move the stone.*
>
> *Move the stone and set it free.*
> *Move the stone, and you will see your miracle.*
> *Move the stone and let it go.*
> *With your faith, it will show your miracle.*
> *Move the stone.*

Lord, why do You wait?
Why do You hesitate?
Where are You, Lord?

Lord, we search the sky of blue,
Lord, we search the sky for You.
Where are You, Lord?

    Again, I heard the words You said,
    It finally settles in my head, move the stone.

    Move the stone and set it free.
    Move the stone, and you will see your miracle.
    Move the stone and let it go.
    With your faith, it will show your miracle.
    Move the stone.

    Just move the stone.

John M. Reichert

AFTERWORD

I pray that God has more songs for me to scribe down. Yet not my will but His. I am willing and still able to serve. Send me a song, and I will write it down for the total Honor and Glory of You, my Lord and Savior!!

My beautiful wife Audrey on Flattop Mountain, 12324 feet, in Rocky Mountain National Park.

*My son Zachary at Lake of the Clouds,
11,400 feet. Rocky Mountain National Park.*

*My daughter Erin, her husband Tim,
and five of my grandchildren.
Isaac, Gabe, Nora, Matthias, and Addie, left to right*

*My son Luke in the sombrero!
He's the favorite of the nieces and nephews.*

Son Bill and grandson William ready for the Thanksgiving feast!

*Daughter Monica, her husband Bryan,
and grandchildren Bradyn, Hank, and Nellie
(oldest to youngest).*

Each family member has been an unending inspiration for me. May God's love and grace shine upon you and a host of angels surround you and protect you with the blood of Jesus.

God's River Otter waiting on another song.

CPSIA information can be obtained
at www.ICGtesting.com
Printed in the USA
LVHW050414250523
747946LV00007B/67

9 798887 387680